W9-AHS-417

A MAN OF SINGULAR VIRTUE

1. *Sir Thomas More as the King's Servant*

A MAN OF SINGULAR VIRTUE

being
A Life of Sir Thomas More
by his son-in-law William Roper
and
a selection of More's Letters

Selected, edited and introduced
by
A. L. ROWSE

LONDON
The Folio Society
1980

PRINTED IN GREAT BRITAIN
by W & J Mackay Limited, Chatham
Filmset in 11 point V.I.P. Plantin spaced 1 point

CONTENTS

ILLUSTRATIONS

INTRODUCTION

Dean Swift, a somewhat improbable witness, considered Sir Thomas More as 'the person of the greatest virtue that this kingdom hath ever produced'. Without going into comparatives, we need have no doubt about More's virtue, or the charm of his personality; while the tragic fate that befell him, caught in the trap of revolutionary circumstances and the conflicts of conscience consequent upon them, which are so brutally familiar to us today, recommends him to our sympathy. Whatever we may think of the issues – and they have been mostly presented to us biased in favour of More – it all makes a splendid, touching story.

More had the good fortune of having a beautiful and compassionate biography of him written by an intimate, his son-in-law Roper, which is one of the first of modern classics of biography. No other Tudor figure had such luck, except possibly More's patron, Cardinal Wolsey, whose life was written by *his* intimate, George Cavendish, his gentleman-in-attendance. Both Wolsey and More were great men – More a man of genius and a saint to boot; both caught in the revolution of their time, and in the end its victims.

We cannot here go into the complex issues of that revolution in church and state, or the controversies over the Reformation – today seen in a more rational, ecumenical temper; we have merely to present Roper's *Life* and a selection of More's English letters in perspective, and show how they illuminate and supplement each other.

(i)

William Roper was the husband of More's favourite daughter Margaret, who makes such endearing appearances in both the biography and letters. He was the son of a Kentish lawyer, with property in St Dunstan's, Canterbury, where is the family vault. Born in 1496, Roper lived to the great age (for those days) of over eighty, not dying till 1578, well into the Protestant reign of Elizabeth I. Though a convinced Catholic, he held on to his office as protonotary of King's Bench, under

2. *William Roper, More's son-in-law*

the tolerant Queen, for altogether fifty-four years, resigning it in only the last year of his life to his son Thomas, whose line came to an end in the next century.

Roper wrote his book not long after More's execution in 1535, though it was not published until 1626 in Paris. Margaret died in 1544, leaving him with two sons and three daughters: they were quite well provided for – as he tells us, More had made his settlement on them before his attainder (he was not a lawyer for nothing), and there were the family properties at Eltham and in Canterbury.

Roper's was the first of several biographies of More, by all counts the best and the source of most of the intimate details about his personal and family life. It is a family circle of exceptional charm that is depicted, taking its tone and ultimately its law from the kindly, humorous, inwardly austere master. That does not mean that they were reduced to dull uniformity by the moral and spiritual ascendancy of the master, or by their devotion to him. There is variety in the spectrum all the way from the dedicated spirit of Margaret, closest to her father, to son-in-law Heron with his eye to the main chance, and so to the practical common sense of More's wife, Dame Alice, who thought it nonsense that he should insist on remaining in the Tower, against the will of King and Council, Parliament and all the bishops (except Fisher) in the country.

We do not have to read between the lines to see that Roper himself thought More's course extreme, the sacrifice of his family unnecessary; and even Margaret, who fully shared her father's religious devotion, at one point wrote to reproach him. *That* really disturbed him as nothing else did, as we can read from his reply to her; he did not take his wife's salutary sagacity seriously, merely put her off with, 'Is not this house [the Tower] as nigh heaven as mine own?'

The atmosphere of More's circle comes through with singular clarity and level-headedness. We appreciate Roper's own religious spirit, his candour and honesty. We are indebted to him not only for his portrayal of personal characteristics; we learn from him, for example, that Henry VIII made More Lord Chancellor partly in the hope of recruiting his aid in the appalling tangle of his matrimonial problem. The King was also a victim of ineluctable circumstances – though, like Stalin, he managed to maintain his control throughout the revolution, whatever the cost. Henry VIII *had* to beget a son to ensure the succession to the throne – Queen Catherine was beyond it – and the son had to be legitimate, to quell any doubt or the possibility of civil war. Roper tells us that Wolsey hoped for a French marriage-alliance and had not contemplated a *mésalliance* with Anne Boleyn. (Nor had anybody but Anne herself, to begin with: when, after years of waiting for her on Henry's part, she became pregnant, Henry thought that here was his chance of a son, and married her.)

For so bull-headed, capricious and impulsive a man, Henry's patience in waiting to marry Anne was remarkable. So, too, was his patience with More: he went on hoping for years to get More's support in his trouble. More was personally a favourite: the disappointment was all the more bitter.

Roper tells us that the Duke of Norfolk was a particular friend to More, and tried to get him to be more obliging to the King. When he realized that this was hopeless and that More was obdurate, the Duke managed to get the King's permission for him to resign the Chancellorship – Henry did not dismiss him, he still went on hoping. From More's relations with Norfolk it would seem that he owed his promotion to the highest office in the land to the Duke. This, the third Duke, was the son of the Surrey we read about in the *Letters,* who had been in the council-chamber in the Tower on the day of Richard III's *coup d'état* and summary execution of Hastings: an eye-witness from whom More could have got a first-hand account for his *Edward V*.

For ourselves, centuries afterward, we can savour the ironies of history and high politics. Henry VIII was as much deceived of his hopes in making More Chancellor, as Henry II had been in making his Chancellor Thomas Becket, Archbishop of Canterbury, expecting that he would do his will in the Church. An even more bitter fate was in store for Anne Boleyn, for her life came to depend upon her rival's: once Catherine was dead, Henry could make a clearance of Anne and an indubitably legitimate marriage – as he did, and at last (though he had left it very late) produced the longed-for son.

Here Roper records for us More's clairvoyance as to Anne's fate, even at the height of her apparent prosperity. More and Henry knew each other pretty intimately, as we see from the *Letters* as well as the *Life*. The saint had no illusions: if his head would purchase the King a castle in France, it should not fail to fall. For all Henry's regal courtesy, which we see displayed in the *Letters*, the undoubted charm he could exert, he was above all (as Napoleon described himself) *un être politique* – a *faux bonhomme,* exactly like his Yorkist grandfather, Edward IV. Henry's father, the Tudor Henry VII, had no charm, and Roper tells us that More when a young MP incurred his severe displeasure for opposing his tax-demands – which the King revenged upon More's father. Roper's veracity, like More's, in that truth-telling circle, is unimpeachable, and his portrayal of Henry VIII's familiarity with his Councillor is fully borne out by the *Letters.* But Roper may have underestimated the rewards More received for his services; in addition to the cash payments we hear about in the *Letters*, he got considerable grants of land in Oxfordshire and Kent, which were resumed upon his attainder. Roper admits that not everybody considered Sir Thomas so wholly virtuous, and royal service anyway enabled him to build his fine residence by the Thames at Chelsea, desirable enough for a duke (Suffolk) to cast envious eyes upon it after his fall. Even then some emoluments from the state continued. The *Letters* enable us to see the relations of complete confidence that subsisted between Wolsey and More. There seems to be no independent confirmation of any such breach between them over the tax-demands from the Parliament of 1523; More's position as Speaker may account for the posture Roper says he took up at the Cardinal's intrusion into the House, perhaps a matter of form and custom rather than of policy.

Upon Wolsey's fall it fell to More as Chancellor to open the historic Reformation Parliament in November 1529, to sign the articles declaring Wolsey guilty of a breach of Praemunire and fining the clergy for their consent to his legatine authority from the Pope. More must have been already uncomfortable in his exalted seat as the new course went forward. But Henry kept him in the office which no layman had ever held before; and in March 1531 it was his duty to announce to the House of Lords the declarations of the universities in favour of the nullity of Henry's marriage. Though the Chancellor refrained from expressing any opinion in public, he had expressed it often enough to the King in private, and his silence was perfectly understood. Next year convocations of the clergy were prohibited without royal licence – a first step in ending the independence of the Church in England and its dependence upon the Papacy; this was followed by a plain threat, a bill to withhold payment of first-fruits to Rome. More could hold out no longer against the new deal as it unfolded from the secular deliberations in Council, upheld by the anti-clerical feeling of the King. Disappointment must have been building up in Henry's mind to a feeling of personal resentment at what, with his absorbing egoism, he would regard as sheer ingratitude.

In May 1532, unable to go along any further, More gave up his office, to Henry's vexation. Roper gives us a charming picture of how More took his release, and how he acted out the part in church to Dame Alice – to her small appreciation, no doubt. He had been Lord Chancellor for only two years and a half, but in that time had built up a reputation as the 'justest judge' Francis Bacon claimed to be later – without his weakness for accepting cash to do good. Also the speediest: he cleared the court of Chancery of arrears of cases; aspersions upon him, as Roper claims, were proved groundless. Purity of intent, however, was of little avail in time of revolution.

Next year, 1533 – the year of Henry's marriage to Anne and procreation of the child that was to be Elizabeth I (Henry had done far better than he knew) – was filled with the lucubrations of a meddlesome nun, the Holy Maid of Kent, who, with an itch for publicity, rent the air with prophecies of doom if the King would not amend his way of life and put away Anne. The Nun of Kent succeeded in getting several excellent persons (including Bishop Fisher) in trouble for listening to her, and contact with her besmirched More. His credulity – and, no doubt, his opposition to the new deal – inclined him to lend her an ear, though he was able to clear himself of any connivance as to political matters. On the Nun's exposure as the impostor she was, he wrote dissociating himself from 'the wicked woman of Canterbury'. Others were less lucky.

3. *Edward VI*

A subject on which Roper lies low is More's persecution of Protestants – of which indeed he was the leading spirit as Councillor and Lord Chancellor. This was in marked contrast to Cardinal Wolsey's tolerant attitude when a little nest of Lutherans was uncovered at his college – to be refounded by Henry as Christ Church. One of these was the distinguished composer, Taverner: 'the Cardinal, for his music, excused him, saying he was but a musician; and so he escaped.' More, however, personally searched the house of a friend in the City, John Petit, for Protestant books, and committed him to prison, where he shortly died before he could be charged. 'An inoffensive leatherseller', John Tewkesbury was burnt just before Christmas 1531 – of whom More wrote, 'there was never a wretch, I ween, better worthy.' About the same time More sent James Bainham, a Middle Temple lawyer, to the Tower to be racked, in the hope of getting on the track of others of his persuasion. Forced to abjure his 'errors', he was subsequently burnt as a 'lapsed heretic' shortly before More ceased to be Chancellor.

More's excuse was that he hated the 'heresy' not the 'heretic': he

4. *Elizabeth I, as Princess*

5. *The Burning of a Heretic*

regarded the holders of such convictions as pests in the commonwealth. But this was precisely as Henry and his Council and Parliament came to regard More as being, obstinately holding to his convictions about Papal supremacy against the consensus of opinion in the country. So much for men's mutually exclusive opinions: it was six of one side to half-a-dozen of the other, as Dame Alice thought, with her woman's point of view against men's intellectual certainties. When More was examined at Lambeth, and Cranmer tried to save him, More was ready to swear to the succession of Anne's children, but not to the oath renouncing the Pope. The Abbot of Westminster reproved him for setting up his own private judgment against the wisdom of the nation, as expressed by Parliament and Council. And this is what it came to. More was thereupon committed to the Abbot's custody and, after the failure of Cranmer to save him, dispatched to the Tower. Even then, Roper tells us, Henry might not have proceeded to the final measures against him if it had not been for the nagging of Anne Boleyn. (Only a year more, and then her turn came.)

But one can see, from the *Life* and the *Letters* alike, how much More longed for martyrdom. He had his wish, like his predecessor long before as Chancellor, Thomas Becket – who thereby became the best known of medieval Englishmen (he was a pure Norman) to the world – whose example meant much to More. As he wrote to Margaret in his last letter: 'I would be sorry if it should be any longer than tomorrow: for it is St Thomas' Even and the utas [octave] of St Peter, and therefore tomorrow long I to go to God – it were a day very meet and convenient for me.'

Before that short sharp journey from the scaffold there had to be the great scene in Westminster Hall, where More had often presided in his glory as Lord Chancellor, for he was indicted of high treason under the Act of Supremacy. (Actually, in the tug-of-war over centuries between the Papacy and the Crown, between Rome and the nation, the Kings of England had usually had the power in the last resort over the Church, though not in matters of faith and doctrine; so the final transference – as with the Parliament Act of 1911 – was less cataclysmic than it sounded.)

In the course of More's several examinations by the ablest members of Henry's Council they had not been able to get out of the cleverest lawyer in England a straight answer on the question at issue: he was not going to accuse himself to make things easy for them. They tried him every way, by kindness, by flattery – asking the prisoner to sit with them as he had so often done in Council – by threats of the King's displeasure, then offers of renewed favour, followed by stricter imprisonment, taking away books, pens, and paper so that he could write briefly to Margaret only with a piece of charcoal. Towards the end More seems to have closed his shutters and shut himself up in darkness to meditate on the next world. But on an informal visit by the Solicitor-General, Rich, with two others, he tried to trap More with a loaded question which he evaded.

At the trial Rich perjured himself by twisting More's answer into a direct denial of the King's Supremacy. There followed the most magnificent snub in English history. 'In faith, Master Rich, I am sorrier for your perjury than for mine own peril. Neither I, nor no man else to my knowledge ever took you to be a man of such credit as in any matter of importance I, or any other, would at any time vouchsafe to communicate with you . . . For we long dwelled in one parish together, where, as yourself can tell, you were esteemed very light of your tongue, a great dicer, and of not commendable fame . . . Can it therefore seem likely unto your honourable lordships that I would, in so weighty a cause, so far overshoot myself as to trust Master Rich – a man of me always reputed for one of so little truth – so far above my sovereign lord the King, or any of his noble Councillors, that I would unto him utter the secrets of my conscience: the special point and only mark at my hands so long sought for? A thing which I never did, nor never would – after the Statute thereof made – reveal it, either to the King's highness himself, or to any of his honourable Councillors.'

6. *Richard III*

Rich's companions said that they had not heard the crucial exchange. Nevertheless More's condemnation was a foregone conclusion; everybody knew what his position was, indeed his opposition – he had several times expressed it to the King himself. And again – one of the ironies of history – when More had in the glad old days been helping Henry with his book against Luther, he had warned the King against putting the Papal claims too highly. (In return the Pope had conferred on Henry the title of 'Defender of the Faith', which he stuck to after his denial of the Papal claims and handed on to his successors to this day.)

The jury at Westminster had no difficulty in reaching their conclusion: they at once pronounced More guilty. Before pronouncing judgment, Lord Chancellor Audley allowed More to speak out, whereupon he came clean and traversed the whole course decided upon by the nation through King, Council, and Parliament, bishops and all. He said outright that the Act of Parliament was 'directly oppugnant to the laws of God and his holy Church, the supreme government of which, or of any part thereof . . .' belonged to the see of Rome. The Act was therefore 'in law amongst Christian men insufficient to charge any Christian'.

Here at last was the direct argument at stake, the cause of the collision. More died simply for the Papal Supremacy. The most brilliant brain in England, the most famous Englishman of the day, was – in modern parlance – a dissident.

Solicitor-General Rich had his reward. He made an enormous fortune, built himself a grand mansion out of the former Leez priory in Essex, remained a faithful Catholic into the Protestant reign of Anne Boleyn's daughter, died in the bosom of the Roman Church and sleeps soundly on his heavy tomb at Felsted. His descendants were Puritan opponents of another king, Charles I, in the Civil War.

(ii)

What is the clue to it all?

That More's career and fate presented a problem was evident to everybody. It was summed up by a representative Englishman of the time, the chronicler Edward Hall, who wrote, 'Surely this was the foolishest wise man, or the wisest foolish man?'

Many answer simply that it was just a case of conscience. But there were plenty of people on the other side who had a conscience too, and thought More wrong. There was Cranmer for one, who had tried to save him, and who ultimately died for *his* conscience.

More's was a complex personality, divided by inner conflict – as is often the case with genius – which in the end, getting towards his term, he resolved in this way. But it had always been there, from the time of intense religious excitement which befell him on reaching manhood, which, as psychologists know, not infrequently occurs with remarkable men.

More, a clever, engaging boy, had had a happy and successful youth at school and in the household of Cardinal Morton at Lambeth, the wise and politic prelate who knew all the secrets of the Wars of the Roses, of Edward IV and Richard III, the sage adviser of respectable Henry VII, the cleric whom More held in esteem all his life. The youth was brought up very religiously; but before coming of age he underwent a prolonged spiritual crisis which made him long for the austerity of the Carthusian life. For four years he subjected himself to its rigours, without making up his mind (he had too much mind to make up). He rose early, took part in the monastic devotions daily, and gave himself up to 'vigils, fasts, prayers, and similar austerities'. He always wore 'a sharp shirt of hair next his skin, which he never left off wholly'; he often scourged himself, when his hair-shirt was bloodstained he gave it to Margaret to wash. (What did his second wife, her stepmother, think of this? A good, brisk housekeeper, she can hardly have held with these ways.)

Once, the young man thought even of taking the vows of a Franciscan. Then, suddenly, this phase came to an end, and More decided on the life of the world, and a worldly career. He married Jane Colt, though somewhat oddly, for she was the eldest daughter whom he did not fancy, when he really fancied her younger sister. Conscience, however, told him that it would humiliate the elder to be passed over for the younger. So he married Jane. When she died after four children in six years, More married again within a month of her death. Evidently, with his vigorous personality, he had some reason for scourging himself and his frequent assertions of sinfulness, his nagging consciousness of sin and expressions of penitence. In truth, all the evidence shows that he was an exceedingly good man; it was merely that he had an excessively sensitive, perhaps an obsessive, conscience.

He was very conscious, too, of worldliness and constantly reproaching himself of it. Here was the conflict; for the humanists, of whom Erasmus and he were the leading lights, all insisted on the duty of serving the state, making their public contribution to the life of the community. (On the other side, it is highly unlikely that Erasmus would have offered himself for martyrdom for any cause whatever.) How valuable More's service was we see from his public career. Few men were so qualified by ability and acumen, education, knowledge of languages, diplomatic finesse, tact, charm, genius for friendship. All these More possessed: they not only drew the attention and favour of Wolsey and Henry but More himself could not but be conscious of his fitness for public service and his duty to perform it. And there were the worldly rewards: promotion inevitably, knighthood (when such things were an honour), the rise to the highest eminence in the land as Lord Chancellor.

But always underneath the robes of office, the great gold chain, there was the hair-shirt. He continued his life of exceptional discipline and religious devotion; then as the crisis grew, his defence of the Church turned into persecution of dissidents and coarse and bitter controversy with no holds barred. The times waxed cruel; it was a sad descent from the golden hopes of the earlier reformers, of Colet and More and Erasmus, to a Europe divided from top to bottom – something we can appreciate from the disaster and wreck of our own time.

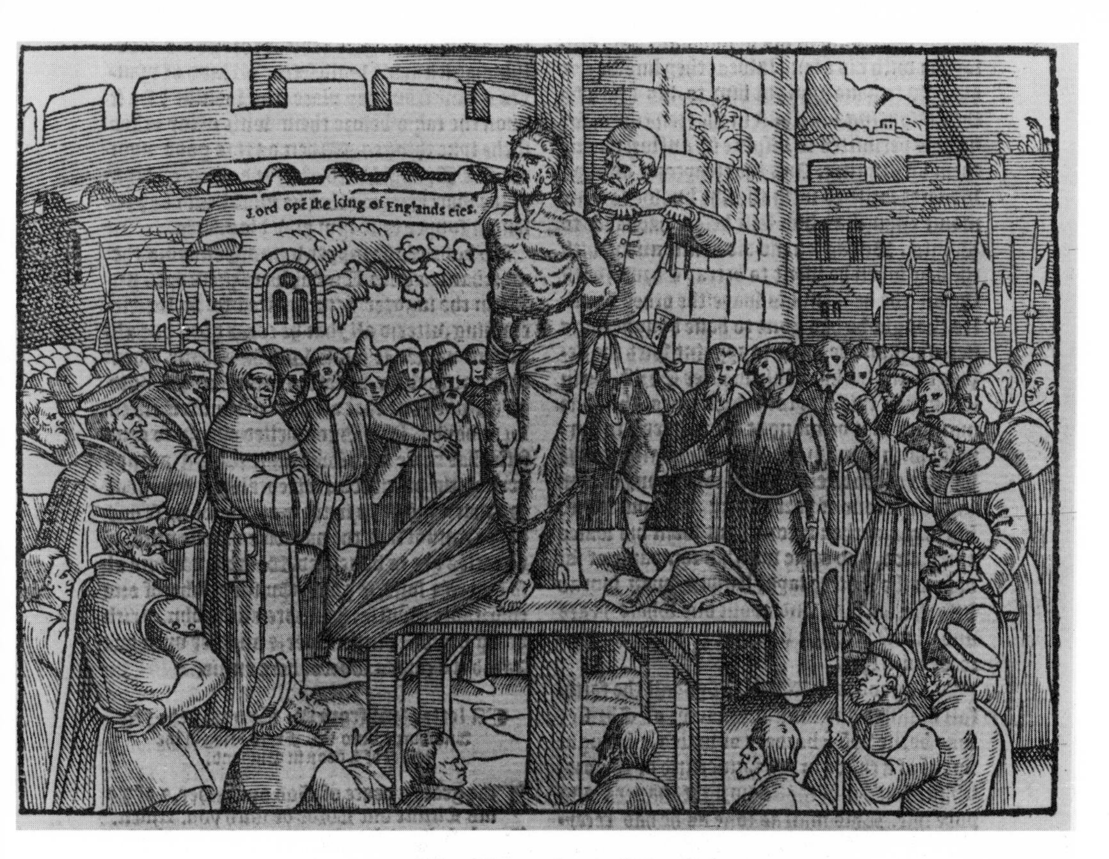

7. *The Martyrdom of Tyndale*

Two phases of More's life are well lighted for us – the earlier and the last. A charm lies upon the early years, which we can catch from Erasmus' letters or an old classic like Seebohm's *Oxford Reformers*. This brilliant circle of Oxford men – Colet and Grocyn, Linacre and Leland, William Latimer and Lily – looked to the reform of religious institutions, the Church and monasticism, universities and schools, the spread of the new humanism, Greek and scriptural knowledge: they did not envisage revolution, dispersal and break-up. Leland, who travelled all over England recording what he could of the monasteries before their destruction, and their libraries before their shocking dispersal, ended up off his head – as others lost theirs. Tyndale, best of Biblical scholars and translators, and More's most eminent target, migrated from Oxford to Cambridge – a significant move – and then into exile in Flanders, where he was strangled. The second generation of English humanists were apt to be Cambridge men and Protestants: Elizabeth I was taught by them, as her sister Mary had been by the earlier Oxford group. They had a brief come-back under her rule, when the splendid tome of More's *Works* was published.

8. *Erasmus*

9. *Dean Colet*

The last phase of his life is, of course, illuminated for us by Roper's biography. But the intervening period of More's public life, far the longest – some twenty years of service to the Crown – is much less well realized by us. Here is the importance of the *Letters,* of which we give as fairly representative a selection of those in English as can be.

Most of More's correspondence is in Latin – naturally, for he was a European figure and Latin was the international language of the time. One notes an occasional piquancy in More's usage: he writes to scholarly clerics, like Archbishop Lee of York or Bishop Tunstall of Durham, in Latin. But his letters to Wolsey are in English – the

10. *Sir Thomas More*

Cardinal's Latin, under the insufferable burden of business all those years, must have become rather rusty; and More wrote to the King in English, for though Henry was an educated man (his love-letters to Anne are in French) and an accomplished musician, he was not a scholar *pur sang* (Anne's daughter was).

The influence of being educated entirely in Latin is obvious in the English of both More and Roper: the long sentences with their convoluted construction, the dependent clauses, the parentheses, the pauses, then beginning again. In both alike one notices the moral, and even legal, scrupulousness, the qualifications, the care to get every statement precisely right, or to specify when they are reporting what they had heard. This makes both of them not easy to read at length. It is necessary to break up the winding sentences by modern punctuation, occasionally explaining, though without changing a word. For they get there in the end: the words and phrases, no less than the scenes themselves, are vivid and telling in spite of the wordiness.

11. *Title page of* Utopia

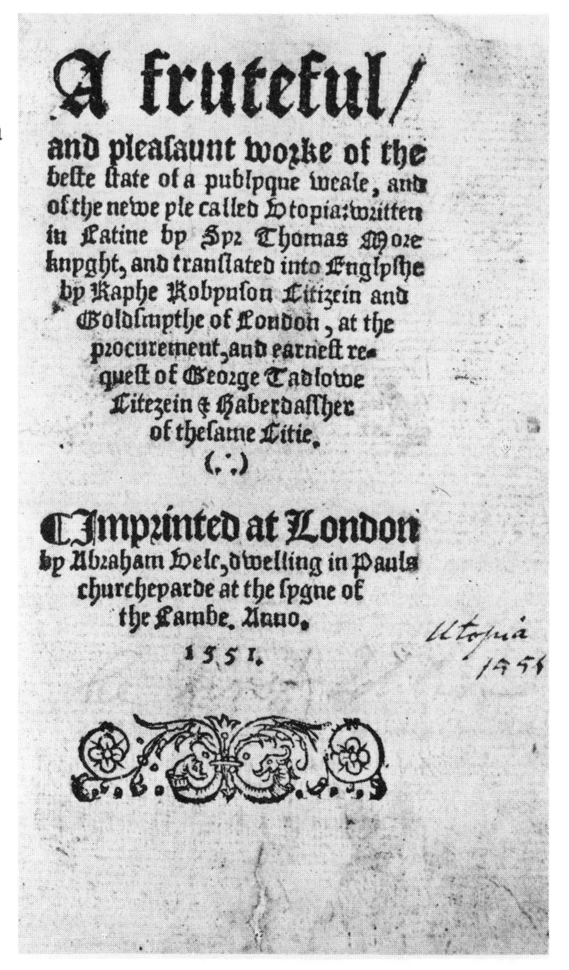

A fruteful/
and pleasaunt worke of the
beste state of a publyque weale, and
of the newe yle called Utopia: written
in Latine by Syr Thomas More
knyght, and translated into Englyshe
by Raphe Robynson Citizein and
Goldsmythe of London, at the
procurement, and earnest request of George Tadlowe
Citezein & Haberdassher
of the same Citie.
(.:.)
Imprinted at London
by Abraham Vele, dwelling in Pauls
churcheyarde at the sygne of
the Lambe. Anno.
1551.

Utopia
1551

More's *Letters* fill out and corroborate Roper's *Life*, but naturally they give us much information and add many touches of their own. We begin with only one public letter, that dedicating his translation of the *Life of Pico della Mirandola*, from his earlier period – about 1505, the year of his marriage – to illustrate his humanist interests, though we see in it his even deeper engagement with religion. Alas that there is no English letter commenting on his *Utopia*, the humanist masterpiece of this early period. Begun in Antwerp on one of his many diplomatic missions abroad, it was written in Latin, the most influential book in its way to have been written by an Englishman in that century.

The *Letters* give us fascinating close-ups of Henry in action; we see upon what confidential terms More was with the King, discussing the troubles of his sister, Queen Margaret, in Scotland. We note Henry's regal courtesy, his consideration for Wolsey, along with his self-confidence – advising him to leave off taking so many medicines and then his health, he assures him, will improve. Or on a diplomatic matter upon which Wolsey and the King had been outsmarted: Wolsey could now see that Henry had foreseen it and told him so, 'whereby he thinketh your grace will the better trust his conjecture hereafter'. We have Henry's concern for the matrimonial chances of his nobles, in the case of his Yorkist cousin, Henry Courtenay, Earl of Devon, subsequently executed. (Henry's character deteriorated with the strains and pressures upon him.) We hear him expressing his obsessive desire for conquest in France – Henry had almost as much French blood as English – and to turn out Francis I as his own father, Henry VII, had turned out his great-uncle Richard III. We even hear Henry's sharp, incisive 'Ha!', remembered into the Elizabethan age and picked up by Shakespeare, who picked up everything.

Letters to the Nun of Kent and to Cromwell bespeak other sides to More's personality and concerns. We have only one to his wife, Dame Alice, and that is cool enough: he is more concerned with the losses to their neighbours than with their own from the fire at Chelsea. His letters to Margaret, full of tenderness and love, yet unyielding on the martyrdom for which he longs, need no comment: they are beyond praise.

The *Letters*, like the *Life*, have their own dramatic interest: one sees the net closing in upon him, drawn by himself. There is the psychological interest, the paradox of genius.

A. L. ROWSE

A Life of Sir Thomas More by William Roper

*In hoc + signo vinces**

Forasmuch as Sir Thomas More, knight, sometime Lord Chancellor of England, a man of singular virtue and of a clear unspotted conscience (as witnesseth Erasmus) more pure and white than the whitest snow, and such an angelical wit, as England (he saith) never had the like before, nor never shall again, universally, as well in the laws of our own realm (a study in effect able to occupy the whole life of a man) as in all other sciences, right well studied, was in his days accounted a man worthy of perpetual famous memory: I, William Roper, though most unworthy, his son-in-law by marriage to his eldest daughter, knowing at this day no man living that of him and of his doings understood so much as myself, for that I was continually resident in his house by the space of sixteen years and more, thought it therefore my part to set forth such matters touching his life as I could at this present call to remembrance. Among which things, very many notable things (not meet to have been forgotten) through negligence and long continuance of time are slipped out of my mind. Yet, to the intent the same should not all utterly perish, I have at the desire of divers worshipful friends of mine (though very far from the grace and worthiness of them, nevertheless as far forth as my mean wit, memory and knowledge would serve me) declared so much thereof as in my poor judgment seemed worthy to be remembered.

This Sir Thomas More – after he had been brought up in the Latin tongue at St Anthony's in London – was by his father's procurement received into the house of the right reverend, wise and learned prelate, Cardinal Morton. Where, though he was young of years, yet would he at Christmas-tide suddenly sometimes step in among the players, and never studying for the matter, make a part of his own there presently among them, which made the lookers-on more sport than all the players

* In this sign thou shalt win the victory.

12. *More's Admission to Doctors' Commons*

Thomas Morus

beside. In whose wit and towardness the Cardinal much delighting, would often say of him unto the nobles that divers times dined with him, 'This child here waiting at the table, whosoever shall live to see it, will prove a marvellous man.'

Whereupon for his better furtherance in learning, he placed him at Oxford, where, when he was both in the Greek and Latin tongue sufficiently instructed, he was then for the study of the law of the realm, put to an Inn of Chancery called New Inn, where for his time he very well prospered. And from thence was admitted to Lincoln's Inn, with very small allowance, continuing there his study until he was made and accounted a worthy utter barrister.

After this, to his great commendation, he read for a good space a public lecture of St Augustine's *De Civitate Dei,* in the Church of St Lawrence in the Old Jewry, whereunto there resorted Doctor Grocyn an excellent cunning* man, and all the chief learned of the City of London.

Then was he made Reader at Furnival's Inn, so remaining by the space of three years and more.

Marriage

After which time he gave himself to devotion and prayer in the Charterhouse of London, religiously living there, without vow, about four years. Until he resorted to the house of one Master Colt, a gentleman of Essex, that had oft invited him thither, having three daughters, whose honest conversation and virtuous education provoked him there specially to set his affection. And albeit his mind most served him to the

* learned.

go · T · Morus 2° die decembris A° A christo nato ...
... Admissus sū in hanc societatē et pollicēor
... solutur̄ū in Annos singulos · f · 6 · s · 8 ·

second daughter, for that he thought her the fairest and best favoured – yet when he considered that it would be both great grief and some shame also to the eldest to see her younger sister in marriage preferred before her, he then of a certain pity framed his fancy towards her. And soon after married her; never the more discontinuing his study of the law at Lincoln's Inn, but applying still the same until he was called to the Bench, and had read twice, which is as often as ordinarily any Judge of the law doth read.

Before which time he had placed himself and his wife at Bucklersbury in London; where he had by her three daughters and one son, in virtue and learning brought up from their youth, whom he would often exhort to take virtue and learning for their meat, and play for their sauce.

Who, ere ever he had been reader in court, was in the latter time of King Henry VII made a burgess of the Parliament. Wherein there were by the King demanded (as I have heard reported) about three fifteenths for the marriage of his eldest daughter that then should be the Scottish Queen. At the last debating whereof he made such arguments and reasons there against, that the King's demands thereby were clean overthrown. So that one of the King's Privy Chamber named Master Tyler, being present thereat, brought word to the King out of the Parliament House that a beardless boy had disappointed all his purpose. Whereupon the King, conceiving great indignation towards him, could not be satisfied until he had some way revenged it. And, forasmuch as he nothing having, nothing could lose, his grace devised a causeless quarrel against his father, keeping him in the Tower until he had made him pay to him an hundred pounds fine.

13. *Henry VII*

Shortly thereupon it fortuned that this Sir Thomas More, coming in a suit to Doctor Fox, Bishop of Winchester (one of the King's Privy Council), the Bishop called him aside, and – pretending great favour towards him – promised him that, if he would be ruled by him, he would not fail into the King's favour again to restore him. Meaning (as it was after conjectured) to cause him thereby to confess his offence against the King, whereby His Highness might with the better colour have occasion to revenge his displeasure against him. But when he had come from the Bishop, he fell in communication with one Master Whitford, his familiar friend, then chaplain to that Bishop, and after a Father of Syon, and showed him what the Bishop had said unto him, desiring to have his advice therein. Who for the Passion of God, prayed him in no wise to follow his counsel; 'For my lord, my master,' quoth he, 'to serve the King's turn, will not stick to agree to his own father's

14. *Henry VII's Queen*

death.' So Sir Thomas More returned to the Bishop no more. And had not the King soon after died, he was determined to have gone over the sea, thinking that being in the King's indignation, he could not live in England without great danger.

After this he was made one of the under-sheriffs of London, by which office and his learning together (as I have heard him say) he gained without grief not so little as four hundred pounds by the year. Since there was at that time in none of the Prince's courts of the laws of this realm, any matter of importance in controversy wherein he was not with the one part of counsel. Of whom for his learning, wisdom, knowledge and experience, men had such estimation that, before he came to the service of King Henry VIII – at the suit and instance of the English merchants – he was, by the King's consent, made twice Ambassador in certain great causes between them and merchants of the

15. *Henry VIII*

Steelyard. Whose wise and discreet dealing therein, to his high commendation, coming to the King's understanding, provoked His Highness to cause Cardinal Wolsey (then Lord Chancellor) to procure him to his service. And albeit the Cardinal, according to the King's request, earnestly travailed* with him therefore, among many other his persuasions alleging him how dear his service must needs be unto His Majesty, which could not, with his honour, with less than he should yearly lose thereby, seem to recompense him. Yet he, loath to change his estate, made such means to the King, by the Cardinal, to the contrary, that His Grace, for that time, was well satisfied.

In favour with the King

Now happened there after this, a great ship of his that then was Pope to arrive at Southampton, which the King claiming for a forfeiture, the Pope's Ambassador, by suit unto His Grace, obtained that he might for his master the Pope have counsel learned in the laws of this realm; and the matter in his own presence (being himself a singular† civilian) in some public place to be openly heard and discussed. At which time there could none of our law be found so meet to be of counsel with this

* laboured. † particularly learned in Civil Law.

16. *Queen Catherine of Aragon*

Ambassador as Sir Thomas More, who could report to the Ambassador in Latin all the reasons and arguments by the learned counsel on both sides alleged. Upon this the counsellors of either part, in presence of the Lord Chancellor, and other the Judges, in the Star Chamber had audience accordingly. Where Sir Thomas More not only declared to the Ambassador the whole effect of all their opinions, but also, in defence of the Pope's side, argued so learnedly himself, that was the aforesaid forfeiture to the Pope restored, and himself among all the hearers, for his upright and commendable demeanour therein, so greatly renowned, that for no entreaty would the King from thenceforth be induced any longer to forbear his service. At whose first entry thereunto, he made him Master of the Requests (having then no better room void) and within a month after knight, and one of his Privy Council.

And so from time to time was he by the Prince advanced, continuing in his singular favour and trusty service twenty years and above. A good part whereof used the King upon holy-days, when he had done his devotions, to send for him into his travers,* and there sometime in matters of astronomy, geometry, divinity and such other faculties, and sometimes of his worldly affairs, to sit and confer with him. And other whiles would he, in the night, have him up into his leads,† there for to

* private study. † flat roof covered with lead.

consider with him the diversities, courses, motions and operations of the stars and planets.

And because he was of a pleasant disposition, it pleased the King and the Queen, after the Council had supped, at the time of their supper, for their pleasure, commonly to call for him to be merry with them. When he perceived so much in his talk to delight, that he could not once in a month get leave to go home to his wife and children (whose company he most desired) and to be absent from the court two days together, but

that he should be thither sent for again, he – much misliking this restraint of his liberty – began thereupon somewhat to dissemble his nature; and so by little and little from his former accustomed mirth to disuse himself, that he was of them from thenceforth at such seasons no more so ordinarily sent for.

Then died one Master Weston, Treasurer of the Exchequer, whose office, after his death, the King of his own offer, without any asking, freely gave unto Sir Thomas More.

17, 18. *Henry VIII at a Tournament*

Speaker of the House of Commons

In the fourteenth year of his grace's reign was there a Parliament holden, whereof Sir Thomas More was chosen Speaker; who, being very loath to take that room upon him, made an oration (not now extant) to the King's highness for his discharge thereof; whereunto when the King would not consent, he spake unto his grace in form following:

'Since I perceive, most redoubted sovereign, that it standeth not with your high pleasure to reform this election and cause it to be changed, but have by the mouth of the most reverend father in God, the Legate, your Highness's Chancellor, thereunto given your most royal assent, and have of your benignity determined, far above that I may bear, to enable me and for this office to repute me meet – rather than you should seem to impute unto your Commons that they have unmeetly chosen – I am therefore, and always shall be, ready obediently to conform myself to the accomplishment of your high commandment, in my most humble wise beseeching your most noble Majesty that I may with your grace's favour, before I farther enter thereunto, make mine humble intercession unto your Highness for two lowly petitions: the one privately concerning myself, the other the whole assembly of your Commons' House.

'For myself, gracious sovereign, that if it mishap me in anything hereafter that is on the behalf of your Commons in your high presence to be declared, to mistake my message, and in the lack of good utterance, by my misrehearsal, to pervert or impair their prudent instructions, it may then like your most noble Majesty, of your abundant grace, with the eye of your accustomed pity, to pardon my simpleness; giving me leave to repair again to the Commons' House, and there to confer with them, and to take their substantial advice what thing and in what wise I shall on their behalf utter and speak before your noble grace. To the intent their prudent devices* and affairs be not by my simpleness and folly hindered or impaired. Which thing, if it should so mishap, as it were well likely to mishap in me – if your gracious benignity relieved not my oversight – it could not fail to be during my life a perpetual grudge and heaviness to my heart, the help and remedy whereof, in manner aforesaid remembered is, most gracious sovereign, my first lowly suit and humble petition unto your most noble grace.

'Mine other humble request, most excellent Prince, is this: forasmuch as there be of your Commons, here by your high commandment assembled for your Parliament, a great number which are, after the

* concerns.

19. *Henry VIII in Parliament*

20. *Henry VIII as a Young Man*

accustomed manner appointed in the Common House to treat and advise of the common affairs among themselves apart, and albeit, most dear liege Lord, that according to your prudent advice, by your honourable writs everywhere declared, there hath been as due diligence used in sending up to your highness's court of Parliament the most discreet persons out of every quarter that men could esteem meet thereunto. Whereby it is not to be doubted but that there is a very substantial assembly of right wise and politic persons. Yet, most victorious Prince, since among so many wise men neither is every man wise alike, nor among so many men, like well witted, every man like well spoken, and it often happeneth that, likewise as much folly is uttered with painted polished speech, so many, boisterous and rude in language, see deep indeed, and give right substantial counsel; and since also in matters of great importance, the mind is often so occupied in the matter that a man rather studieth what to say than how, by reason whereof the wisest man and the best spoken in a whole country fortuneth among, while his mind is fervent in the matter, somewhat to speak in such wise as he would afterward wish to have been uttered otherwise, and yet no worse will had when he spake it, than he hath when he would so gladly change it: therefore, most gracious sovereign, considering that in your high court of Parliament is nothing entreated but matter of weight and importance concerning your realm and your own royal estate, it could not fail to let* and put to silence from the giving of their advice and counsel many of your discreet Commons, to the great hindrance of the common affairs, except that every of your Commons were utterly discharged of all doubt and fear how anything that it should happen them to speak, should happen of your highness to be taken.

'And in this point, though your well known and proved benignity putteth every man in right good hope. Yet such is the weight of the matter, such is the reverend dread that the timorous hearts of your natural subjects conceive toward your high majesty, our most redoubted King and undoubted sovereign, that they cannot in this point find themselves satisfied, except your gracious bounty therein declared put away the scruple of their timorous minds, and animate and encourage them, and put them out of doubt. It may therefore like your most abundant grace, our most benign and godly King, to give to all your Commons here assembled your most gracious licence and pardon, freely, without doubt of your dreadful displeasure, every man to discharge his conscience, and boldly in everything incident among us to

* hinder.

21. *Cardinal Wolsey*

declare his advice. And whatsoever happen any man to say, that it may like your noble majesty, of your inestimable goodness, to take all in good part, interpreting every man's words, how uncunningly* soever they be couched, to proceed yet of good zeal towards the profit of your realm and honour of your royal person. The prosperous estate and preservation whereof, most excellent sovereign, is the thing which we all, your most humble loving subjects, according to the most bounden duty of our natural allegiance, most highly desire and pray for.'

Cardinal Wolsey

At this Parliament Cardinal Wolsey found himself much grieved with the Burgesses thereof, for that nothing was so soon done or spoken therein but that it was immediately blown abroad in every alehouse. It fortuned at that Parliament a very great subsidy to be demanded, which the Cardinal fearing would not pass the Common House, determined for the furtherance thereof to be there personally present himself. Before whose coming, after long debating therein, whether it were better but with a few of his lords (as the most opinion of the House was) or with his whole train royally to receive him there amongst them.

'Masters,' quoth Sir Thomas More, 'forasmuch as my Lord Cardinal lately, you wot† well, laid to our charge the lightness of our tongues for things uttered out of this House, it shall not in my mind be amiss with all his pomp to receive him, with his maces, his pillars, his poleaxes, his crosses, his hat, and Great Seal too, to the intent, if he find the like fault with us hereafter, we may be the bolder from ourselves to lay the blame on those that his Grace bringeth hither with him.' Whereunto the House wholely agreeing, he was received accordingly.

Where, after that he had in solemn oration by many reasons proved how necessary it was the demand there moved to be granted, and further showed that less would not serve to maintain the Prince's purpose, he – seeing the company sitting still silent, and thereunto nothing answering, and contrary to his expectation showing in themselves towards his request no towardness of inclination – said unto them, 'Masters, you have many wise and learned men among you, and since I am from the King's own person sent hither unto you for the preservation of yourselves and the realm, I think it meet you give me some reasonable answer.' Whereat, every man holding his peace, then began he to speak to one Master Marney (after Lord Marney). 'How say you,' quoth he, 'Master Marney?' Who making no answer neither, he

* ignorantly. † know.

severally asked the same question of divers others accounted the wisest of the company.

To whom, when none of them all would give so much as one word, being before agreed, as the custom was, by their Speaker to make answer, 'Masters,' quoth the Cardinal, 'unless it be the manner of your House, as of likelihood it is, by the mouth of your Speaker, whom you have chosen for trusty and wise, as indeed he is, in such cases to utter your minds, here is without doubt a marvellous obstinate silence.'

And thereupon he required an answer of Master Speaker, who – first reverently upon his knees excusing the silence of the House, abashed at the presence of so noble a personage, able to amaze the wisest and best learned in a realm, and after by many probable arguments proving that for them to make answer was it neither expedient nor agreeable with the ancient liberty of the House – in conclusion for himself showed that though they had all with their voices trusted him, yet except every one of them could put into his one head all their several wits, he alone in so weighty a matter was unmeet to make his grace answer.

Whereupon the Cardinal, displeased with Sir Thomas More, that had not in this Parliament in all things satisfied his desire, suddenly arose and departed.

After the Parliament ended, in his gallery at Whitehall in Westminster, uttered unto him his griefs, saying, 'Would to God you had been at Rome, Master More, when I made you Speaker.' 'Your grace not offended, so would I too, my Lord,' quoth he. And to wind such quarrels out of the Cardinal's head, he began to talk of that gallery, and said, 'I like this gallery of yours, my lord, much better than your gallery at Hampton Court.' Wherewith so wisely brake he off the Cardinal's displeasant talk. The Cardinal at that present, as it seemed, wist* not what more to say to him.

But for the revengement of his displeasure, counselled the King to send him Ambassador into Spain, commending to His Highness his wisdom, learning and meetness for that voyage. And the difficulty of the cause considered, none was there, he said, so well able to serve his grace therein. Which, when the King had broken to Sir Thomas More, and that he had declared unto his grace how unfit a journey it was for him, the nature of the country and disposition of his complexion so disagreeing together that he should never be likely to do his grace acceptable service there – knowing right well that if his grace sent him thither, he should send him to his grave; but showing himself nevertheless ready, according to his duty all were it with the loss of his life, to

* knew.

22. *Archbishop Warham*

fulfil his grace's pleasure in that behalf. The King, allowing well his answer, said unto him, 'It is not our meaning, Master More, to do you hurt, but to do you good would we be glad, we will for this purpose devise upon some other, and employ your service otherwise.'

Chancellor of the Duchy of Lancaster

And such entire favour did the King bear him that he made him Chancellor of the Duchy of Lancaster, upon the death of Sir Richard Wingfield, who had that office before.

And for the pleasure he took in his company, would his grace suddenly sometimes come home to his house at Chelsea, to be merry with him. Whither on a time, unlooked for, he came to dinner to him, and after dinner, in a fair garden of his, walked with him by the space of an hour, holding his arm about his neck. As soon as his grace was gone, I, rejoicing thereat, told Sir Thomas More how happy he was whom the King had so familiarly entertained, as I never had seen him do to any other except Cardinal Wolsey, whom I saw his grace once walk with, arm in arm. 'I thank our Lord, son,' quoth he, 'I find his grace my very good lord indeed, and I believe he doth as singularly favour me as any subject within this realm. Howbeit, son Roper, I may tell thee I have no cause to be proud thereof, for if my head could win him a castle in France (for then there was a war between us) it should not fail to go.'

This Sir Thomas More among all other his virtues, was of such meekness that if it had fortuned him with any learned man resorting to him from Oxford, Cambridge or elsewhere, as there did divers – some for desire of his acquaintance, some for the famous report of his wisdom and learning, and some for suits of the universities – to have entered into argument, wherein few were comparable unto him, and so far to have discoursed with them therein that he might perceive they could not, without some inconvenience, hold out much further disputation against him, then, lest he should discomfort them, as he that sought not his own glory, but rather would seem conquered than to discourage students in their studies, ever showing himself more desirous to learn than to teach, would he by some witty device courteously break off into some other matter, or give over.

Of whom, for his wisdom and learning, had the King such an opinion, that at such time as he attended upon his highness, taking his progress either to Oxford or Cambridge, where he was received with very eloquent orations, his grace would always assign him, as one that was prompt and ready therein, *ex tempore* to make answer thereunto. Whose manner was, whensoever he had occasion, either here or beyond the sea, to be in any University, not only to be present at the reading and disputation there commonly used, but also learnedly to dispute among them himself.

Who, being Chancellor of the Duchy, was made ambassador twice, joined in commission with Cardinal Wolsey, once to the Emperor Charles into Flanders, the other time to the French King into France.

Not long after this, the Water-bailiff of London, sometime his servant, hearing, where he had been at dinner, certain merchants liberally to rail against his old master, waxed so discontented therewith that he hastily came to him and told him what he had heard. 'And were I you, sir,' quoth he, 'in such favour and authority with my Prince as you are, such men surely should not be suffered so villainously and falsely to misreport and slander me. Wherefore I would wish you to call them before you, and to their shame for their lewd malice punish them.'

Who, smiling upon him, said, 'Why, Master Water-bailiff, would you have me punish those by whom I receive more benefit than by you all that be my friends? Let them a' God's name speak as lewdly as they list of me, and shoot never so many arrows at me, as long as they do not hit me, what am I the worse? But if they should once hit me, then would it indeed not a little trouble me. Howbeit I trust, by God's help, there shall none of them all once be able to touch me. I have more cause, I assure thee, Master Water-bailiff, to pity them than to be angry with them.' Such fruitful communication had he oftentimes with his familiar friends.

So on a time, walking with me along the Thames side at Chelsea, in talking of other things he said unto me, 'Now would to our Lord, son Roper, upon condition that three things were well established in Christendom, I were put into a sack, and here presently cast into the Thames.'

'What great things be those, sir,' quoth I, 'that should move you so to wish?'

'Wouldst thou know what they be, son Roper?' quoth he.

'Yea, marry, with good will, sir, if it please you,' quoth I.

'In faith, son, they be these,' said he. 'The first is, that where the most part of Christian princes be at mortal war, they were all at an universal peace. The second, that where the Church of Christ is at present sore afflicted with many errors and heresies, it were settled in a perfect uniformity of religion. The third, that where the King's matter of his marriage is now come in question, it were to the glory of God and quietness of all parties brought to a good conclusion.' Whereby, as I could gather, he judged that otherwise it would be a disturbance to a great part of Christendom.

Thus did it by his doings throughout the whole course of his life

appear that all his travail and pains, without respect of earthly commodities, either to himself, or any of his, were only upon the service of God, the Prince, and the realm, wholly bestowed and employed. Whom I heard in his later time to say that he never asked the King himself the value of one penny.

Devotional Life

As Sir Thomas More's custom was daily, if he were at home, besides his private prayers, with his children to say the seven psalms, litany and suffrages following, so was his guise nightly, before he went

23. *The More Family*

to bed, with his wife, children and household to go to his chapel and there upon his knees ordinarily to say certain psalms and collects with them. And because he was desirous for godly purposes sometime to be solitary, and sequester himself from worldly company, a good distance from his mansion house builded he a place called the New Building, wherein there was a chapel, a library and a gallery. In which, as his use was upon other days to occupy himself in prayer and study together, so on the Friday there usually continued he from morning till evening, spending his time only in devout prayers and spiritual exercises.

24. *Three Generations of the More Family*

And to provoke his wife and children to the desire of heavenly things, he would sometimes use these words unto them:

'It is now no mastery* for you children to go to heaven, for everybody giveth you good counsel, everybody giveth you good example; you see virtue rewarded and vice punished, so that you are carried up to heaven even by the chins. But if you live the time that no man will give you good counsel, nor no man will give you good example, when you shall see virtue punished and vice rewarded, if you will then stand fast and firmly stick to God, upon pain of life, though you be but half good, God will allow you for the whole.'

If his wife or any child had been diseased or troubled, he would say unto them, 'We may not look at our pleasure to go to heaven in feather-beds; it is not the way. For our Lord himself went thither with

* victory.

great pain and by many tribulations; which was the path wherein he walked thither, for the servant may not look to be in better case than his master.'

And as he would in this sort persuade them to take their troubles patiently, so would he in like sort teach them to withstand the devil and his temptations valiantly, saying,

'Whosoever will mark the devil and his temptations shall find him therein much like to an ape. For like as an ape, not well looked unto, will be busy and bold to do shrewd turns, and contrariwise, being spied, will suddenly leap back and adventure no farther, so the devil, finding a man idle, slothful and without resistance ready to receive his temptations, waxeth so hardy that he will not fail still to continue with him, until to his purpose he have throughly brought him. But on the other side, if he see a man with diligence persevere to prevent and withstand his temptations, he waxeth so weary that in conclusion he utterly forsaketh him. For as the devil of disposition is a spirit of so high a pride that he cannot abide to be mocked, so is he of nature so envious that he feareth any more to assault him, lest he should thereby not only catch a foul fall himself, but also minister to the man more matter of merit.'

Thus delighted he evermore not only in virtuous exercises to be occupied himself, but also to exhort his wife, children and household to embrace and follow the same.

To whom, for his notable virtue and godliness, God showed, as it seemed, a manifest miraculous token of his special favour towards him. At such time as my wife, as many other that year were, was sick of the sweating sickness; who, lying in so great extremity of that disease as by no invention or devices that physicians in such cases commonly use (of whom she had divers both expert, wise and well learned, then continually attendant about her) she could be kept from sleep – so that both physicians and all other there despaired of her recovery, and gave her over. Her father, as he that most entirely tendered her, being in no small heaviness for her, by prayer at God's hand sought to get her a remedy.

Whereupon going up, after his usual manner, into his aforesaid New Building, there in his chapel, upon his knees, with tears most devoutly besought Almighty God that it would like his goodness, unto whom nothing was impossible, if it were his blessed will, at his mediation to vouchsafe graciously to hear his humble petition. Where incontinent came into his mind that a glister* should be the only way to help her. Which, when he told the physicians, they by and by confessed that, if

* clyster: enema.

there were any hope of health, that was the very best help indeed, much marvelling of themselves that they had not before remembered it.

Then was it immediately ministered unto her sleeping, which she could by no means have been brought unto waking. And albeit after that she was thereby thoroughly awaked, God's marks, an evident undoubted token of death, plainly appeared upon her; yet she, contrary to all expectation was, as it was thought, by her father's fervent prayer miraculously recovered, and at length again to perfect health restored. Whom, if it had pleased God at that time to have taken to his mercy, her father said he would never have meddled with worldly matters after.

Now while Sir Thomas More was Chancellor of the Duchy, the see of Rome chanced to be void, which was cause of much trouble. For Cardinal Wolsey, a man very ambitious, and desirous (as good hope and likelihood he had) to aspire unto that dignity, perceiving himself of his expectation disappointed, by means of the Emperor Charles so highly commending one Cardinal Adrian, sometime his schoolmaster, to the Cardinals of Rome, in the time of their election, for his virtue and worthiness, that thereupon was he chosen Pope. Who from Spain, where he was then resident, coming on foot to Rome, before his entry into the city, did put off his hose and shoes, barefoot and barelegged passing through the streets towards his palace, with such humbleness that all the people had him in great reverence. Cardinal Wolsey, I say, waxed* so wood† therewith, that he studied to invent all ways of revengement of his grief against the Emperor, which, as it was the beginning of a lamentable tragedy, so some part of it as not impertinent to my present purpose, I reckoned requisite here to put in remembrance.

The King's Marriage

This Cardinal therefore, not ignorant of the King's inconstant and mutable disposition, soon inclined to withdraw his devotion from his own most noble, virtuous and lawful wife, Queen Katherine, aunt to the Emperor, upon every light occasion. And upon other, to her in nobility, wisdom, virtue, favour and beauty, far incomparable, to fix his affection – meaning to make this his so light disposition an instrument to bring about his ungodly intent – devised to allure the King (then already, contrary to his mind, nothing less looking for, falling in love with the Lady Anne Boleyn) to cast fancy to one of the French King's sisters. Which thing, because of the enmity and war that was at that time between the French King and the Emperor (whom, for the

* grew. † angry.

25. *Catherine of Aragon*

cause afore remembered, he mortally maligned) he was very desirous to procure. And for the better achieving thereof, requested Longland, Bishop of Lincoln, and ghostly father* to the King, to put a scruple into his grace's head, that it was not lawful for him to marry his brother's wife.

Which the King, not sorry to hear of, opened it first to Sir Thomas More, whose counsel he required therein, showing him certain places of Scripture that somewhat seemed to serve his appetite. Which, when he had perused, and thereupon as one that had never professed the study of divinity, himself excused to be unmeet many ways to meddle with such matters. The King, not satisfied with this answer, so sore still pressed upon him therefore, that in conclusion he condescended to his grace's motion. And further, forasmuch as the case was of such importance as needed great advisement and deliberation, he besought his grace of sufficient respite advisedly to consider of it. Wherewith the King, well contented, said unto him that Tunstall and Clark, Bishops of Durham and Bath, with other learned of his Privy Council, should also be dealers therein.

So Sir Thomas More departing, conferred those places of Scripture with expositions of divers of the old holy doctors, and at his coming to the Court, in talking with his grace of the aforesaid matter, he said:

'To be plain with your grace, neither my Lord of Durham, nor my Lord of Bath, though I know them both to be wise, virtuous, learned and honourable prelates, nor myself, with the rest of your Council, being all your grace's own servants, for your manifold benefits daily bestowed on us so most bounden to you, be, in my judgment, meet counsellors for your grace herein. But if your grace mind to understand the truth, such counsellors may you have devised, as neither for respect of their own worldly commodity, nor for fear of your princely authority, will be inclined to deceive you.' To whom he named then St Jerome, St Augustine and divers other old holy doctors, both Greeks and Latins, and moreover showed him what authorities he had gathered out of them. Which although the King (as disagreeable with his desire) did not very well like of, yet were they by Sir Thomas More, who in all his communication with the King in that matter had always most discreetly behaved himself, so wisely tempered, that he both presently took them in good part, and oft-times had thereof conference with him again.

After this were there certain questions among his Council propounded, whether the King needed in this case to have any scruple at all,

* confessor.

and if he had, what way were best to be taken to deliver him of it. The most part of whom were of opinion that there was good cause of scruple, and that for discharging of it, suit were meet to be made to the see of Rome. Where the King hoped by liberality to obtain his purpose; wherein, as it after appeared, he was far deceived.

Then was there for the trial and examination of this matrimony procured from Rome a commission in which Cardinal Campeggio and Cardinal Wolsey were joined commissioners who for the determination thereof, sat at the Blackfriars in London. Where a libel* was put in for the annulling of the said matrimony, alleging the marriage between the King and Queen to be unlawful. And for proof of the marriage to be lawful, was there brought in a dispensation, in which, after divers disputations thereon holden, there appeared an imperfection. Which, by an instrument or brief, upon search found in the Treasury of Spain, and sent to the commissioners in England, was supplied. And so should judgment have been given by the Pope accordingly, had not the King, upon intelligence thereof, before the same judgment, appealed to the next General Council. After whose application the Cardinal upon that matter sat no longer.

It fortuned before the matter of the said matrimony brought in question, when I, in talk with Sir Thomas More, of a certain joy commended unto him the happy estate of this realm that had so catholic a Prince that no heretic durst show his face, so virtuous and learned a clergy, so grave and sound a nobility, and so loving, obedient subjects, all in one faith agreeing together.

'True it is indeed, son Roper,' quoth he, and in commending all degrees and estates of the same went far beyond me.'And yet, son Roper, I pray God', said he, 'that some of us, as high as we seem to sit upon the mountains, treading heretics under our feet like ants, live not the day that we gladly would wish to be at league and composition with them, to let them have their churches quietly to themselves, so that they would be content to let us have ours quietly to ourselves.' After that I had told him many considerations why he had no cause so to say, 'Well,' said he, 'I pray God, son Roper, some of us live not till that day,' showing me no reason why he should put any doubt therein. To whom I said, 'By my troth, sir, it is very desperately spoken.' That vile term, I cry God mercy, did I give him. Who, by these words, perceiving me in a fume, said merrily unto me, 'Well, well, son Roper, it shall not be so, it shall not be so.' Whom in sixteen years and more being in house conversant with him, I could never perceive as much as once in a fume.

* plea.

26. *Henry VIII*

But now to return again where I left. After the supplying of the imperfections of the dispensation sent (as before rehearsed) to the commissioners into England, the King, taking the matter for ended – and then meaning no farther to proceed in that matter – assigned the

27. *Queen Anne Boleyn*

Bishop of Durham and Sir Thomas More to go ambassadors to Cambrai, a place neither Imperial nor French, to treat a peace between the Emperor, the French King and him. In the concluding whereof Sir Thomas More so worthily handled himself, procuring in our league far more benefits unto this realm than at that time by the King or his Council was thought possible to be compassed, that for his good service in that voyage, the King, when he after made him Lord Chancellor, caused the Duke of Norfolk openly to declare unto the people (as you

shall hear hereafter more at large) how much all England was bound unto him.

Now upon the coming home of the Bishop of Durham and Sir Thomas More from Cambrai, the King was as earnest in persuading Sir Thomas More to agree unto the matter of his marriage as before, by many and divers ways provoking him thereunto. For the which cause, as it was thought, he the rather soon after made him Lord Chancellor, and further declaring unto him that, though at his going over sea to Cambrai he was in utter despair thereof, yet he had conceived since some good hope to compass it. For albeit his marriage, being against the positive laws of the Church and the written laws of God, was holpen* by the dispensation, yet was there another thing found out of late, he said, whereby his marriage appeared to be so directly against the law of nature that it could in no wise by the Church be dispensable. As Doctor Stokesley (whom he then preferred to be Bishop of London, and in that case chiefly credited) was able to instruct him, with whom he prayed him in that point to confer. But for all his conference with him, he saw nothing of such force as could induce him to change his opinion therein; which notwithstanding the Bishop showed himself in his report of him to the King's highness so good and favourable that he said he found him

* helped.

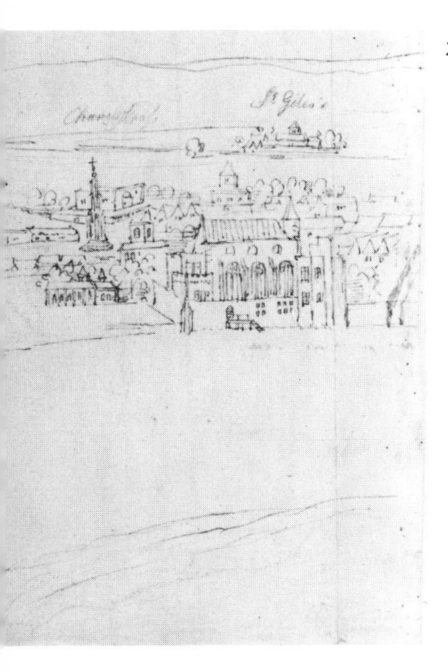

28. *More's Westminster*

in his grace's cause very toward, and desirous to find some good matter wherewith he might truly serve his grace to his contentment.

Lord Chancellor

This Bishop Stokesley, being by the Cardinal not long before in the Star Chamber openly put to rebuke and awarded to the Fleet, not brooking his contumelious usage, and thinking that forasmuch as the Cardinal – for lack of such forwardness in setting forth the King's divorce as his grace looked for, was out of his highness's favour – he had now a good occasion offered him to revenge his quarrel against him: further to incense the King's displeasure towards him, busily travailed to invent some colourable device for the King's furtherance in that behalf. Which (as before is mentioned) he to his grace revealed, hoping thereby to bring the King to the better liking of himself, and the more misliking of the Cardinal. Whom his highness therefore soon after of his office displaced, and to Sir Thomas More, the rather to move him to incline to his side, the same in his stead committed.

Who, between the Dukes of Norfolk and Suffolk, being brought through Westminster Hall to his place in the Chancery, the Duke of Norfolk, in audience of all the people there assembled, showed that he was from the King himself straightly charged, by special commission, there openly, in the presence of them all, to make declaration how much

29. *Henry VIII in Parliament*

all England was beholding to Sir Thomas More for his good service. And how worthy he was to have the highest room in the realm, and how dearly his grace loved and trusted him, for which, said the Duke, he had great cause to rejoice. Whereunto Sir Thomas More, among many other his humble and wise sayings not now in my memory, answered that although he had good cause to take comfort of his highness's singular favour towards him, that he had, far above his deserts, so highly commended him, to whom therefore he acknowledged himself most deeply bounden, yet, nevertheless, he must of his own part needs confess, that in all things by his grace alleged he had done no more than was his duty. And further disabled himself as unmeet for that room; wherein, considering how wise and honourable a prelate had lately before taken so great a fall, he had, he said, thereof no cause to rejoice. And as they had before, on the King's behalf, charged him uprightly to minister indifferent justice to the people, without corruption or affection, so did he likewise charge them again, that if they saw him at any time, in any thing, digress from any part of his duty in that honourable office – even as they would discharge their own duty and fidelity to God and the King – so should they not fail to disclose it to his grace, who otherwise might have just occasion to lay his fault wholly to their charge.

While he was Lord Chancellor, being at leisure (as seldom he was), one of his sons-in-law on a time said merrily unto him, 'When Cardinal Wolsey was Lord Chancellor, not only divers of his privy chamber, but such also as were his doorkeepers got great gain.' And since he had married one of his daughters, and gave still attendance upon him, he thought he might of reason look for some; where he indeed, because he was so ready himself to hear every man, poor and rich, and kept no doors shut from them, could find none, which was to him a great discouragement. And whereas else, some for friendship, some for kindred, and some for profit, would gladly have had his furtherance in bringing them to his presence, if he should now take anything of them, he knew, he said, he should do them great wrong; for that they might do as much for themselves as he could do for them. Which condition, although he thought in Sir Thomas More very commendable, yet to him, being his son, he found it nothing profitable.

When he had told his tale: 'You say well, son,' quoth he. 'I do not mislike that you are of conscience so scrupulous, but many other ways be there, son, that I may both do yourself good and pleasure your friend also. For sometime may I by my word stand your friend in stead,* and

* in help.

sometime may I by my letter help him; or if he have a cause depending before me, at your request I may hear him before another. Or if his cause be not all the best, yet may I move the parties to fall to some reasonable end by arbitrament. Howbeit, this one thing, son, I assure thee on my faith, that if the parties will at my hands call for justice, then, all were it my father stood on the one side and the devil on the other, his cause being good, the devil should have right.' So offered he his son, as he thought, he said, as much favour as with reason he could require.

And that he would for no respect digress from justice, well appeared by a plain example of another of his sons-in-law called Master Heron. For when he, having a matter before him in Chancery, and presuming too much of his favour, would by him in no wise be persuaded to agree to any indifferent order, then made he in conclusion a flat decree against him.

This Lord Chancellor used commonly every afternoon to sit in his open hall, to the intent that, if any persons had suit unto him, they might the more boldly come to his presence and there open their complaints before him. Whose manner was also to read every bill himself, ere he would award any subpoena, which bearing matter sufficient worthy a subpoena, would he set his hand unto or else cancel it.

Whensoever he passed through Westminster Hall to his place in the Chancery by the court of the King's Bench, if his father, one of the judges thereof, had been sat ere he came, he would go into the same court, and there reverently kneeling down in the sight of them all, duly ask his father's blessing. And if it fortuned that his father and he, at readings in Lincoln's Inn, met together, as they sometimes did, notwithstanding his high office, he would offer in argument the pre-eminence to his father, though he, for his office' sake, would refuse to take it. And for the better declaration of his natural affection towards his father, he not only, while he lay on his death-bed, according to his duty, oft times with comfortable words most kindly came to visit him, but also at his departure out of the world with tears taking him about the neck, most lovingly embraced him, commending him into the merciful hands of Almighty God, and so departed from him.

And so few injunctions* as he granted while he was Lord Chancellor, yet were they by some of the judges of the law misliked, which I understanding declared the same to Sir Thomas More, who answered me that they should have little cause to find fault with him therefore.

* Restraining writs.

30. *More's Father*

31. *A Drawing of More*

And thereupon caused he one Master Crooke, chief of the six clerks, to make a docket containing the whole number and causes of all such injunctions as either in his time had already passed, or at that present depended in any of the King's courts at Westminster before him. Which done, he invited all the judges to dine with him in the Council Chamber at Westminster, where, after dinner, when he had broken with them what complaints he had heard of his injunctions and moreover showed them both the number of causes of every one of them, in order, so plainly that, upon full debating of those matters, they were all enforced to confess that they, in like case, could have done no otherwise themselves. Then offered he this unto them, that if the justices of every court (unto whom the reformation of the rigour of the law, by reason of their office, most especially appertained) would, upon reasonable considerations, by their own discretions (as they were, he thought, in conscience bound), mitigate and reform the rigour of the law themselves, there should from thenceforth by him no more injunctions be granted.

Whereunto when they refused to condescend, then said he unto them, 'Forasmuch as yourselves, my lords, drive me to that necessity for awarding out injunctions to relieve the people's injury, you cannot hereafter any more justly blame me.' After that he said secretly unto me, 'I perceive, son, why they like not so to do, for they see that they may by the verdict of the jury cast off all quarrels from themselves upon them, which they account their chief defence, and therefore am I compelled to abide the adventure of all such reports.'

Defender of Orthodoxy

And as little leisure as he had to be occupied in the study of holy scripture and controversies upon religion and such other virtuous exercises, being in manner continually busied about the affairs of the King and the realm, yet such watch and pain in setting forth of divers profitable works, in defence of the true Christian religion, against heresies secretly sown abroad in the realm, assuredly sustained he, that the Bishops, to whose pastoral cure the reformation thereof principally appertained, thinking themselves by his travail, wherein by their own confession they were not able with him to make comparison, of their duties in that behalf discharged. And considering that for all his Prince's favour he was no rich man, nor in yearly revenues advanced as his worthiness deserved, therefore at a convocation among themselves and other of the clergy, they agreed together and concluded upon a sum of four or five thousand pounds, at the least, to my remembrance, for his pains to recompense him. To the payment whereof every bishop, abbot and rest of the clergy were, after the rate of their abilities, liberal contributories, hoping this portion should be to his contentation.

Whereupon Tunstall, Bishop of Durham, Clark, Bishop of Bath, and, as far as I can call to mind, Veysey, Bishop of Exeter, repaired unto him, declaring how thankfully his travails, to their discharge, in God's cause bestowed, they reckoned themselves bound to consider him. And that albeit they could not, according to his deserts, so worthily as they gladly would, requite him therefore, but must reserve that only to the goodness of God, yet for a small part of recompense, in respect of his estate so unequal to his worthiness, in the name of their whole convocation, they presented unto him that sum, which they desired him to take in good part.

Who, forsaking it, said, that like as it was no small comfort unto him that so wise and learned men so well accepted his simple doings, for which he never intended to receive reward but at the hands of God only, to whom alone was the thanks thereof chiefly to be ascribed, so gave he most humble thanks to their honours all for their so bountiful and friendly consideration.

When they, for all their importunate pressing upon him, that few would have went* he could have refused it, could by no means make him to take it, then besought they him to be content yet that they might bestow it upon his wife and children. 'Not so, my lords,' quoth he, 'I had liefer† see it all cast into the Thames than I, or any of mine, should have thereof the worth of one penny. For though your offer, my lords, be indeed very friendly and honourable, yet set I so much by my pleasure and so little by my profit, that I would not, in good faith, for so much, and much more too, have lost the rest of so many nights' sleep as was spent upon the same. And yet wish would I, for all that, upon condition that all heresies were suppressed, that all my books were burned and my labour utterly lost.'

Thus departing, were they fain to restore unto every man his own again.

Mortifications

This Lord Chancellor, albeit he was to God and the world well known of notable virtue (though not so of every man considered) yet, for the avoiding of singularity, would he appear none otherwise than other men in his apparel and other behaviour. And albeit outwardly he appeared honourable like one of his calling, yet inwardly he no such vanities esteeming, secretly next his body wore a shirt of hair: which my sister

* thought. † rather.

More,* a young gentlewoman, in the summer, as he sat at supper, singly in his doublet and hose, wearing thereupon a plain shirt, without ruff or collar, chancing to spy it, began to laugh at it. My wife, not ignorant of his manner, perceiving the same, privily told him of it, and he, being sorry that she saw it, presently amended it.

He used also sometimes to punish his body with whips, the cords knotted, which was known only to my wife, his eldest daughter, whom for her secrecy above all other he specially trusted, causing her, as need required, to wash the same shirt of hair.

Now shortly upon his entry into the high office of the Chancellorship, the King yet eftsoons again moved him to weigh and consider his great matter: who, falling down upon his knees, humbly besought his highness to stand his gracious sovereign, as he ever since his entry into his grace's service had found him, saying there was nothing in the world had been so grievous unto his heart as to remember that he was not able, as he willingly would, with the loss of one of his limbs, for that matter anything to find whereby he could, with his conscience, safely serve his grace's contentation. As he that always bare in mind the most godly words that his highness spake unto him at his first coming into his noble service, the most virtuous lesson that ever prince taught his servant, willing him first to look unto God, and after God to him. As, in good faith, he said, he did, or else might his grace well account him his most unworthy servant. To this the King answered, that if he could not therein with his conscience serve him, he was content to accept his service otherwise, and using the advice of other of his learned Council, whose consciences could well enough agree therewith, would nevertheless continue his gracious favour towards him, and never with that matter molest his conscience after.

Resignation

But Sir Thomas More, in process of time, seeing the King fully determined to proceed forth in the marriage of Queen Anne, and when he, with the bishops and nobles of the higher House of the Parliament, were, for the furtherance of that marriage, commanded by the King to go down to the Commons' House to show unto them both what the universities, as well as of other parts beyond the seas as of Oxford and Cambridge, had done in that behalf, and their seals also testifying the same – all which matters, at the King's request, not showing of what mind himself was therein, he opened to the lower House of the Parliament. Nevertheless, doubting lest further attempts after should follow,

* Anne Cresacre, wife of John More, the son of Sir Thomas.

which – contrary to his conscience, by reason of his office, he was likely to be put unto – he made suit unto the Duke of Norfolk, his singular dear friend, to be a means to the King that he might, with his grace's favour, be discharged of that chargeable* room of the Chancellorship, wherein, for certain infirmities of his body, he pretended himself unable any longer to serve.

This Duke, coming on a time to Chelsea to dine with him, fortuned to find him at the church, singing in the choir, with a surplice on his back; to whom, after service, as they went homeward together, arm in arm, the Duke said, 'God body! God body! My Lord Chancellor, a parish clerk, a parish clerk! You dishonour the King and his office.' 'Nay,' quoth Sir Thomas More, smiling upon the Duke, 'your grace may not think that the King, your master and mine, will with me, for serving of God, his master, be offended, or thereby count his office dishonoured.'

When the Duke, being thereunto often solicited, by importunate suit had at length of the King obtained for Sir Thomas More a clear discharge of his office, then, at a time convenient, by his highness's appointment, repaired he to his grace, to yield up unto him the great seal. Which, as his grace, with thanks and praise for his worthy service in that office, courteously at his hands received, so pleased it his highness further to say unto him – that for the service that he before had done him, in any suit which he should after have unto him, that either should concern his honour (for that word it liked his highness to use unto him) or that should appertain unto his profit, he should find his highness good and gracious lord unto him.

After he had thus given over the Chancellorship, and placed all his gentlemen and yeomen with bishops and noblemen, and his eight watermen with the Lord Audley, that in the same office succeeded him – to whom also he gave his great barge – then, calling us all that were his children unto him, and asking our advice how we might now, in this decay of his ability (by the surrender of his office so impaired that he could not, as he was wont, and gladly would, bear out the whole charges of them all himself) from thenceforth be able to live and continue together, as he wished we should. When he saw us silent, and in that case not ready to show our opinions to him, 'Then will I', said he, 'show my poor mind unto you. I have been brought up', quoth he, 'at Oxford, at an Inn of Chancery, at Lincoln's Inn and also in the King's Court, and so forth from the lowest degree to the highest, and yet have I in yearly revenues at this present left me little above an hundred pounds

* burdensome.

32. *The Duke of Norfolk*

by the year, so that now must we hereafter, if we like to live together, be contented to become contributories together. But, by my counsel, it shall not be best for us to fall to the lowest fare first. We will not therefore descend to Oxford fare, nor to the fare of New Inn, but we will begin with Lincoln's Inn diet, where many right worshipful and of good years do live full well; which, if we find not ourselves the first year able to maintain, then will we the next year go one step down to New Inn fare, wherewith many an honest man is well contented. If that exceed our ability too, then will we the next year after descend to Oxford fare, where many grave, learned and ancient fathers be continually conversant. Which if our power stretch not to maintain neither, then may we yet with bags and wallets, go a begging together, and hoping that for pity some good folk will give us their charity, at every man's door to sing *Salve Regina*,* and so still keep company and be merry together.'

And whereas you have heard before, he was by the King from a very worshipful living taken into his grace's service, with whom, in all the great and weighty causes that concerned his highness or the realm, he consumed and spent with painful cares, travels and troubles, as well beyond the seas as within the realm, in effect the whole substance of his life; yet with all the gain he got thereby, being never wasteful spender thereof, was he not able, after the resignation of his office of Lord Chancellor, for the maintenance of himself and such as necessarily belonged unto him, sufficiently to find meat, drink, fuel, apparel and such other necessary charges. All the land that ever he purchased, which also he purchased before he was Lord Chancellor, was not, I am well assured, above the value of twenty marks by the year. And after his debts paid, he had not, I know, his chain excepted, in gold and silver left him the worth of one hundred pounds.

And whereas upon the holy-days during his high Chancellorship, one of his gentlemen, when service at the church was done, ordinarily used to come to my lady his wife's pew, and say unto her, 'Madame, my lord is gone,' the next holy-day after the surrender of his office and departure of his gentleman, he came unto his lady his wife's pew himself, and making a low curtsy, said unto her, 'Madame, my lord is gone.'

In the time somewhat before his trouble, he would talk with his wife and children of the joys of heaven and the pains of hell, of the lives of holy martyrs, of their grievous martyrdoms, of their marvellous patience, and of their passions and deaths that they suffered rather than they would offend God. And what an happy and blessed thing it was,

* The Latin hymn in honour of the Queen (of Heaven).

for the love of God, to suffer loss of goods, imprisonment, loss of lands and life also. He would further say unto them that, upon his faith, if he might perceive his wife and children would encourage him to die in a good cause, it should so comfort him that for very joy thereof, it would make him merely run to death. He showed unto them afore what trouble might after fall unto him, wherewith and the like virtuous talk he had so long before his trouble encouraged them, that when he after fell into trouble indeed, his trouble to them was a great deal the less. *Quia spicula previsa minus laedunt.**

Now upon this resignment of his office, came Master Thomas Cromwell, then in the King's high favour, to Chelsea to him with a message from the King. Wherein when they had thoroughly communed together, 'Master Cromwell,' quoth he, 'You are now entered into the service of a most noble, wise and liberal Prince. If you will follow my poor advice, you shall, in your counsel giving unto his grace, ever tell him what he ought to do, but never what he is able to do. So shall you show yourself a true faithful servant and a right worthy Councillor. For if a lion knew his own strength, hard were it for any man to rule him.'

Shortly thereupon was there a commission directed to Cranmer, then Archbishop of Canterbury, to determine the matter of the matrimony between the King and Queen Katherine, at St Albans, where, according to the King's mind, it was thoroughly determined. Who, pretending he had no justice at the Pope's hands, from thenceforth sequestered himself from the see of Rome, and so married the Lady Anne Boleyn. Which Sir Thomas More understanding said unto me, 'God give grace, son, that these matters within a while be not confirmed with oaths.' I, at that time seeing no likelihood thereof, yet fearing lest his forespeaking it would the sooner come to pass, waxed therefore for his so saying much offended with him.

Coronation of Queen Anne

It fortuned not long before the coming of Queen Anne through the streets of London from the Tower to Westminster to her coronation, that he received a letter from the Bishops of Durham, Bath and Winchester, requesting him both to keep them company from the Tower to the coronation. And also to take twenty pounds that by the bearer thereof they had sent him to buy him a gown with, which he thankfully receiving, and at home still tarrying, at their next meeting said merrily unto them:

* Because troubles foreseen hurt less.

33. *Archbishop Cranmer*

'My lords, in the letters which you lately sent me, you required two things of me: the one whereof, since I was so well content to grant you, the other therefore I thought I might be the bolder to deny you. And like as the one, because I took you for no beggars, and myself I knew to be no rich man, I thought I might the rather fulfil. So the other did put me in remembrance of an Emperor that had ordained a law that whosoever committed a certain offence (which I now remember not) except it were a virgin, should suffer the pains of death, such a reverence had he for virginity. Now so it happened that the first committer of that offence was indeed a virgin, whereof the Emperor hearing was in no small perplexity, as he that by some example fain would have had that law to have been put in execution. Whereupon when his Council had sat long, solemnly debating this case, suddenly arose there up one of his Council, a good plain man, among them, and said, "Why make you so much ado, my lords, about so small a matter? Let her first be deflowered, and then after may she be devoured." And so though your lordships have in the matter of the matrimony hitherto kept yourselves pure virgins, yet take good heed, my lords, that you keep your virginity still. For some there be that by procuring your lordships first at the coronation to be present, and next to preach for the setting forth of it, and finally to write books to all the world in defence thereof, are desirous to deflower you. And when they have deflowered you then will they not fail soon after to devour you. Now my lords,' quoth he, 'it lieth not in my power but that they may devour me, but God being my good Lord, I will provide that they shall never deflower me.'

The Nun of Kent

In continuance, when the King saw that he could by no manner of benefits win him on his side, then, lo, went he about by terrors and threats to drive him thereunto. The beginning of which trouble grew by occasion of a certain nun dwelling in Canterbury for her virtue and holiness among people not a little esteemed; unto whom, for that cause, many religious persons, Doctors of Divinity, and divers others of good worship of the laity used to resort. Who, affirming that she had revelations from God to give the King warning of his wicked life, and of the abuse of the sword and authority committed unto him by God, and understanding my lord of Rochester, Bishop Fisher, to be a man of notable virtuous living and learning, repaired to Rochester. And there disclosed to him all her revelations, desiring his advice and counsel therein. Which the Bishop perceiving might well stand with the laws of God and his holy Church, advised her (as she before had warning and intended) to go to the King herself, and to let him understand the whole circumstance thereof. Whereupon she went to the King and told him all her revelations, and so returned home again.

And in short space after, she, making a voyage to the nuns of Syon, by means of one Master Reynolds, a father of the same house, there fortuned concerning such secrets as had been revealed unto her (some part whereof seemed to touch the matter of the King's Supremacy and marriage, which shortly thereupon followed) to enter into talk with Sir Thomas More. Who, notwithstanding he might well, at that time, without danger of any law (though after, as himself had prognosticated before, those matters were established and confirmed by oaths) freely and safely have talked with her therein; nevertheless, in all the communication between them (as in process appeared) had always so discreetly demeaned himself that he deserved not to be blamed, but contrariwise to be commended and praised.

Accused of Corruption

And had he not been one that in all his great offices and doings for the King and realm, so many years together, had from all corruption of wrong doing or bribes taking kept himself so clear that no man was able therewith once to blemish him or make just quarrel against him, it would, without doubt, in this troublous time of the King's indignation towards him, have been deeply laid to his charge, and of the King's highness most favourably accepted. As in the case of one Parnell it most manifestly appeared; against whom, because Sir Thomas More, while he was Lord Chancellor, at the suit of one Vaughan, his adversary, had made a decree, this Parnell to his highness most grievously complained that Sir Thomas More, for making the same decree, had of the same Vaughan (unable for the gout to travel abroad himself) by the hands of his wife taken a fair great gilt cup for a bribe. Who thereupon, by the King's appointment, being called before the whole Council, where that matter was heinously laid to his charge, forthwith confessed that forasmuch as that cup was, long after the aforesaid decree, brought him for a New Year's gift, he, upon her importunate pressing upon him therefore, of courtesy, refused not to receive it.

Then the Lord of Wiltshire (for hatred of his religion preferrer* of this suit) with much rejoicing said unto the lords, 'Lo, did I not tell you, my lords, that you should find this matter true?' Whereupon Sir Thomas More desired their lordships that as they had courteously heard him tell the one part of his tale, so they would vouchsafe of their honours indifferently to hear the other. After which obtained, he

* promoter.

further declared unto them that, albeit he had indeed, with much work, received that cup, yet immediately thereupon he caused his butler to fill it with wine, and of that cup drank to her. And that when he had so done, and she pledged him, then as freely as her husband had given it to him, even so freely gave her the same unto her again, to give unto her husband as his New Year's gift. Which, at his instant request, though much against her will, at length yet she was fain to receive, as herself, and certain other there, presently before them deposed. Thus was the great mountain turned scant to a little molehill.

So I remember that at another time, upon a New Year's day, there came to him one Mistress Crocker, a rich widow, for whom, with no small pain, he had made a decree in the Chancery against the Lord Arundel, to present him with a pair of gloves, and forty pounds in angels* in them for a New Year's gift. Of whom he thankfully receiving the gloves, but refusing the money, said unto her, 'Mistress, since it were against good manners to forsake a gentlewoman's New Year's gift, I am content to take your gloves, but as for your money I utterly refuse.' So, much against her mind, enforced he her to take her gold again.

And one Master Gresham likewise, having at the same time a cause depending in the Chancery before him, sent him for a New Year's gift a fair gilt cup, the fashion whereof he very well liking, caused one of his own (though not in his fantasy of so good a fashion, yet better in value) to be brought him out of his chamber: which he willed the messenger, in recompense, to deliver to his master, and under other conditions would he in no wise receive it.

Many things more of like effect, for the declaration of his innocency and clearness from all corruption or evil affection, could I rehearse besides, which for tediousness omitting, I refer to the readers by these few before remembered examples, with their own judgments wisely to weigh and consider the same.

The Bill of Attainder

At the Parliament following was there put into the Lords' House a bill to attaint the Nun and divers other religious persons of high treason, and the Bishop of Rochester, Sir Thomas More and certain others, of misprision of treason. The King presupposing of likelihood that this bill would be to Sir Thomas More so troublous and terrible that it would force him to relent and condescend to his request – wherein his grace was much deceived. To which bill Sir Thomas More was a suitor personally to be received in his own defence to make answer. But the

* gold coins.

King, not liking that, assigned the Archbishop of Canterbury, the Lord Chancellor, the Duke of Norfolk and Master Cromwell, at a day and place appointed, to call Sir Thomas More before them. At which time, I, thinking that I had a good opportunity, earnestly advised him to labour unto those Lords for the help of his discharge out of that Parliament Bill. Who answered me he would.

And at his coming before them, according to their appointment, they entertained him very friendly, willing him to sit down with them, which in no wise he would. Then began the Lord Chancellor to declare unto him how many ways the King had showed his love and favour towards him, how fain he would have had him continue in his office, how glad he would have been to have heaped more benefits upon him, and finally how he could ask no worldly honour nor profit at his highness's hands that were likely to be denied him. Hoping, by the declaration of the King's kindness and affection towards him, to provoke him to recompense his grace with the like again, and unto those things that the Parliament, the bishops and the universities had already passed, to add his consent.

To this Sir Thomas More mildly made answer, saying, 'No man living is there, my lords, that would with better will do the thing that should be acceptable to the King's highness than I, which must needs confess his manifold goodness and bountiful benefits most benignly bestowed on me. Howbeit, I verily hoped that I should never have heard of this matter more, considering that I have, from time to time, always from the beginning, so plainly and truly declared my mind unto his grace which his highness to me ever seemed, like a most gracious prince, very well to accept, never minding, as he said, to molest me more therewith. Since which time any further thing that was able to move me to any change could I never find, and if I could, there is none in all the world that would have been gladder of it than I.'

Many things more were there of like sort uttered on both sides. But in the end, when they saw they could by no manner of persuasions remove him from his former determination, then began they more terribly to touch him, telling him that the King's highness had given them in commandment, if they could by no gentleness win him, in his name with his great ingratitude to charge him, that never was there servant to his sovereign so villainous, nor subject to his prince so traitorous as he. For he, by his subtle sinister slights most unnaturally procuring and provoking him to set forth a book of *The Assertion of the Seven Sacraments* and maintenance of the Pope's authority, had caused him, to his dishonour thoughout all Christendom, to put a sword into the Pope's hands to fight against himself.

34. *Pope Clement VII*

When they had thus laid forth all the terrors they could imagine against him, 'My lords,' quoth he, 'these terrors be arguments for children, and not for me. But to answer that wherewith you do chiefly burden me, I believe the King's highness of his honour will never lay that to my charge. For none is there that can in that point say in my excuse more than his highness himself, who right well knoweth that I never was procurer nor counsellor of his majesty thereunto. But after it was finished, by his grace's appointment and consent of the makers of the same, only a sorter out and placer of the principal matters therein contained. Wherein when I found the Pope's authority highly advanced and with strong arguments mightily defended, I said unto his grace, "I must put your highness in remembrance of one thing, and that is this. The Pope, as your grace knoweth, is a prince as you are, and in league with all other Christian princes. It may hereafter so fall out that your grace and he may vary upon some points of the league, whereupon may grow breach of amity and war between you both. I think it best therefore that that place be amended, and his authority more slenderly touched."

' "Nay," quoth his grace, "that shall it not. We are so much bounden unto the see of Rome that we cannot do too much honour unto it."

'Then did I further put him in remembrance of the Statute of Praemunire, whereby a good part of the Pope's pastoral cure here was pared away.

'To that answered his highness, "Whatsoever impediment be to the contrary, we will set forth that authority to the uttermost. For we received from that see our Crown Imperial"; which, till his grace with his own mouth told it me, I never heard of before. So that I trust, when his grace shall be once truly informed of this, and call to his gracious remembrance my doing in that behalf, his highness will never speak of it more, but clear me thoroughly therein himself.'

And thus displeasantly departed they.

Then took Sir Thomas More his boat towards his house at Chelsea, wherein by the way he was very merry, and for that I was nothing sorry, hoping that he had got himself discharged out of the Parliament bill. When he was landed and come home, then walked we twain alone in his garden together, where I, desirous to know how he had sped, said, 'I trust, sir, that all is well because you be so merry.'

'It is so indeed, son Roper, I thank God,' quoth he.

'Are you then put out of the Parliament bill?' said I.

'By my troth, son Roper,' quoth he, 'I never remembered it.'

'Never remembered it, sir,' said I, 'a case that toucheth yourself so near, and us all for your sake! I am sorry to hear it, for I verily trusted, when I saw you so merry, that all had been well.'

Then said he, 'Wilt thou know, son Roper, why I was so merry?'

'That would I gladly, sir,' quoth I.

'In good faith, I rejoiced, son,' quoth he, 'that I had given the devil a foul fall, and that with those lords I had gone so far, as without great shame I could never go back again.'

At which words waxed I very sad, for though himself liked it well, yet liked it me but a little.

The King's Anger

Now upon the report made by the Lord Chancellor and the other lords to the King of all their whole discourse had with Sir Thomas More, the King was so highly offended with him, that he plainly told them he was fully determined that the aforesaid Parliament bill should undoubtedly proceed forth against him. To whom the Lord Chancellor and the rest of the lords said that they perceived the Lords of the Upper House so precisely bent to hear him in his own defence, make answer himself, that if he were not put out of the bill it would without fail be utterly an overthrow of all. But, for all this, needs would the King have his own will therein, or else he said that at the passing thereof, he would be personally present himself.

Then the Lord Audley and the rest, seeing him so vehemently set thereupon, on their knees most humbly besought his grace to forbear the same, considering that if he should in his own presence receive an overthrow, it would not only encourage his subjects ever after to condemn him, but also throughout all Christendom redound to his dishonour ever. Adding thereunto that they mistrusted not in time against him to find some meeter matter to serve his turn better. For in this case of the Nun, he was accounted, they said, so innocent and clear, that for his dealing therein, men reckoned him far worthier of praise than reproof. Whereupon at length, through their earnest persuasion, he was content to condescend to their petition.

And on the morrow, Master Cromwell, meeting me in the Parliament House, willed me to tell my father that he was put out of the Parliament bill. But because I had appointed to dine that day in London, I sent the message by my servant to my wife to Chelsea. Whereof when she informed her father, 'In faith, Meg' quoth he, '*Quod differtur, non aufertur.*'*

After this, as the Duke of Norfolk and Sir Thomas More chanced to fall in familiar talk together, the Duke said unto him, 'By the Mass, Master More, it is perilous striving with princes. And therefore I would wish you somewhat to incline to the King's pleasure, for, by God's body, Master More, *Indignatio principis mors est.*'†

'Is that all, my Lord?' quoth he. 'Then in good faith is there no more difference between your grace and me, but that I shall die today and you tomorrow.'

Act of Supremacy

So fell it out, within a month or thereabouts after the making of the Statute of the Supremacy and Matrimony, that all the priests of London and Westminster, and no temporal man‡ but he, were sent to appear at Lambeth before the Bishop of Canterbury, the Lord Chancellor and Secretary Cromwell, commissioners appointed there to tender the oath unto them.

Then Sir Thomas More, as his accustomed manner was always, ere he entered into any matter of importance, as when he was first chosen of the King's Privy Council, when he was sent ambassador, appointed Speaker of the Parliament, made Lord Chancellor, or when he took any like weighty matter upon him, to go to church and be confessed, to hear Mass and be howsled,§ so did he likewise in the morning early the selfsame day that he was summoned to appear before the lords at Lambeth. And whereas he evermore used before at his departure from his wife and children, whom he tenderly loved, to have them bring him

* What is put off, is not got rid of. † The wrath of the prince is death.
‡ layman. § receive the sacrament.

to his boat, and there to kiss them all and bid them farewell, then would he suffer none of them forth of the gate to follow him, but pulled wicket after him, and shut them all from him. And with an heavy heart, as by his countenance it appeared, with me and our four servants there took he his boat towards Lambeth. Wherein sitting still sadly a while, at last he suddenly rounded me in the ear, and said, 'Son Roper, I thank our Lord, the field is won.' What he meant thereby I then wist not, yet loath to seem ignorant, I answered, 'Sir, I am thereof glad.' But as I conjectured afterwards, it was for that the love he had to God wrought in him so effectually that it conquered all his carnal affections utterly.

Now at his coming to Lambeth, how wisely he behaved himself before the commissioners, at the ministration of the oath unto him, may be found in certain letters sent to my wife remaining in a great book of his works.* Where by the space of four days he was betaken to the custody of the Abbot of Westminster, during which time the King consulted with his Council what order were meet to be taken with him. And albeit in the beginning they were resolved that with an oath not to be acknowledged whether he had to the Supremacy been sworn, or what he thought thereof, he should be discharged, yet did Queen Anne, by her importunate clamour, so sore exasperate the King against him, that contrary to his former resolution, he caused the said oath of the Supremacy to be administered unto him. Who, albeit he made a discreet qualified answer, nevertheless was forthwith committed to the Tower.

* see later p117.

36. *Traitor's Gate at the Tower*

37. *Lambeth Palace*

The Tower

Whom, as he was going thitherward, wearing, as he commonly did, a chain of gold about his neck, Sir Richard Cromwell, that had the charge of his conveyance thither, advised him to send home his chain to his wife, or to some of his children. 'Nay, sir,' quoth he, 'that I will not, for if I were taken in the field by my enemies, I would they should somewhat fare the better by me.'

At whose landing Master Lieutenant at the Tower gate was ready to receive him, where the Porter demanded of him his upper garment. 'Master Porter,' quoth he, 'here it is,' and took off his cap and delivered it him saying, 'I am sorry it is no better for you.' 'No, sir,' quoth the Porter, 'I must have your gown.'

And so was he by Master Lieutenant conveyed to his lodging, where he called unto him one John à Wood, his own servant, there appointed to attend upon him, who could neither write nor read, and sware him before the Lieutenant that if he should hear or see him, at any time, speak or write any manner of thing against the King, the Council, or the state of the realm, he should open it to the Lieutenant, that the Lieutenant might incontinent reveal it to the Council.

Now when he had remained in the Tower a little more than a month, my wife, longing to see her father, by her earnest suit at length got leave to go to him. At whose coming, after the seven psalms* and litany said (which, whensoever she came to him, ere he fell in talk of any worldly matters, he used accustomably to say with her) among other communication he said unto her, 'I believe, Meg, that they that put me here, ween† they have done me a high displeasure. But I assure thee on my faith, my own good daughter, if it had not been for my wife and you that be my children, whom I account the chief part of my charge, I would not have failed long ere this to have closed myself in as strait a room and straiter too. But since I am come hither without mine own desert, I trust that God of his goodness will discharge me of my care and with his gracious help supply my lack among you. I find no cause, I thank God, Meg, to reckon myself in worse case here than in mine own house. For me thinketh God maketh me a wanton, and setteth me on his lap and dandleth me.' Thus by his gracious demeanour in tribulation appeared it that all the troubles that ever chanced unto him, by his patient sufferance thereof, were to him no painful punishments but of his patience profitable exercises.

And at another time when he had first questioned with my wife awhile of the order of his wife, children and state of his house in his

* Penitential Psalms. † think.

absence, he asked her how Queen Anne did. 'In faith, father,' quoth she, 'never better.' 'Never better! Meg,' quoth he. 'Alas! Meg, alas! It pitieth me to remember into what misery, poor soul, she shall shortly come.'

After this, Master Lieutenant, coming into his chamber to visit him, rehearsed the benefits and friendship that he had many ways received at his hands, and how much bounden he was therefore friendly to entertain him and make him good cheer. Which, since the case standing as it did, he could not do without the King's indignation, he trusted, he said, he would accept his good will, and such poor cheer as he had. 'Master Lieutenant,' quoth he again. 'I verily believe, as you may, so you are my good friend indeed and would, as you say, with your best cheer entertain me; for the which I most heartily thank you, and assure yourself, Master Lieutenant, I do not mislike my cheer; but whensoever I do, then thrust me out of your doors.'

Whereas the oath confirming the Supremacy and Matrimony was by the first statute in few words comprised, the Lord Chancellor and Master Secretary did of their own heads add more words unto it, to make it appear unto the King's ears more pleasant and plausible. And that oath, so amplified, caused they to be ministered to Sir Thomas More, and to all other throughout the realm. Which Sir Thomas More perceiving, said unto my wife, 'I may tell thee, Meg, they that have committed me hither, for refusing of this oath not agreeable to the statute, are not by their own law able to justify my imprisonment. And surely, daughter, it is great pity that any Christian prince should by a flexible Council ready to follow his affections, and by a weak clergy lacking grace constantly to stand to their learning, with flattery be so shamefully abused.' But at length the Lord Chancellor and Master Secretary, espying their own oversight in that behalf, were fain afterwards to find the means that another statute should be made for the confirmation of the oath so amplified with their additions.

After Sir Thomas More had given over his office and all other worldly doings therewith, to the intent he might from thenceforth the more quietly settle himself to the service of God, then made he a conveyance for the disposition of all his lands, reserving to himself an estate thereof only for the term of his own life. And after his decease assuring some part of the same to his wife, some to his son's wife for a jointure, on consideration that she was an inheritrix in possession of more than an hundred pounds land by the year, and some to me and my wife in recompense of our marriage money, with divers remainders over. All which conveyance and assurance was perfectly finished long before that matter whereupon he was attainted was made an offence, and yet after

by statute clearly voided. And so were all his lands that he had to his wife and children by the said conveyance in such sort assured, contrary to the order of law, taken away from them, and brought into the King's hands, saving that portion which he had appointed to my wife and me – which, although he had in the foresaid conveyance reserved as he did the rest for term of life to himself, nevertheless, upon further consideration two days after, by another conveyance, he gave the same immediately to my wife and me in possession. And so because the statute had undone only the first conveyance, giving no more to the King but so much as passed by that, the second conveyance, whereby it was given to my wife and me, being dated two days after, was without the compass of the statute. And so was our portion to us by that means clearly reserved.

Martyrdom of the Carthusians

As Sir Thomas More in the Tower chanced on a time, looking out of his window, to behold one Master Reynolds, a religious, learned and virtuous father of Syon, and three monks of the Charterhouse, for the

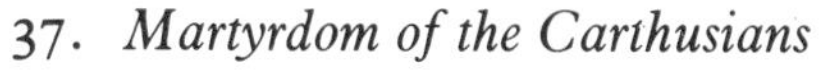

37. *Martyrdom of the Carthusians*

matters of the Matrimony and Supremacy going out of the Tower to execution, he, as one longing in that journey to have accompanied them, said unto my wife then standing there beside him, 'Lo, dost thou not see, Meg, that these blessed fathers be now as cheerfully going to their deaths as bridegrooms to their marriage? Wherefore mayest thou see, mine own good daughter, what a great difference there is between such as have in effect spent all their days in a strait, hard, penitential and painful life religiously, and such as have in the world, like worldly wretches as thy poor father hath done, consumed all their time in pleasure and ease licentiously. For God, considering their long continued life in most sore and grievous penance, will no longer suffer them to remain here in this vale of misery and iniquity, but speedily hence taketh them to the fruition of his everlasting deity. Whereas thy silly father, Meg, that like a most wicked caitiff hath passed forth the whole course of his miserable life most sinfully, God, thinking him not worthy so soon to come to that eternal felicity, leaveth him here yet still in the world, further to be plunged and turmoiled with misery.'

Within a while after, Master Secretary, coming to him into the Tower from the King, pretended much friendship towards him, and for his comfort told him that the King's highness was his good and gracious lord, and minded not with any matter wherein he should have cause of scruple, from henceforth to trouble his conscience. As soon as Master Secretary was gone, to express what comfort he conceived of his words, he wrote with a coal, for ink then had he none, these verses following:

Eye-flattering fortune, look thou never so fair
Nor never so pleasantly begin to smile,
As though thou wouldst my ruin all repair,
During my life thou shalt not me beguile,
Trust I shall God, to enter in a while
His haven of heaven, sure and uniform;
Ever after thy calm look I for no storm.

Lady More's Point of View

When Sir Thomas More had continued a good while in the Tower, my lady, his wife, obtained licence to see him. Who, at her first coming, like a simple ignorant woman, and somewhat worldly too, with this manner of salutation bluntly saluted him:

'What the good year, Master More,' quoth she, 'I marvel that you, that have been always hitherto taken for so wise a man, will now so play the fool to lie here in this close, filthy prison, and be content thus to be shut up amongst mice and rats, when you might be abroad at your liberty. And with the favour and good will both of the King and his Council, if you would but do as all the bishops and best learned of this realm have done. And seeing you have at Chelsea a right fair house, your library, your books, your gallery, your garden, your orchard and all other necessaries so handsome about you, where you might in the company of me your wife, your children and household be merry, I muse what a God's name you mean here still thus fondly to tarry.'

After he had a while quietly heard her, with a cheerful countenance he said unto her, 'I pray thee, good Mistress Alice, tell me one thing.'

'What is that?' quoth she.

'Is not this house', quoth he, 'as nigh heaven as my own?'

To whom she, after her accustomed homely fashion, not liking such talk, answered, 'Tilly-vally, tilly-vally!'

'How say you, Mistress Alice,' quoth he, 'is it not so?'

'Bone deus, bone deus,* man, will this gear† never be left?' quoth she.

* Good God. † stuff.

'Well then, Mistress Alice, if it be so,' quoth he, 'it is very well. For I see no great cause why I should much joy either of my gay house or of anything belonging thereunto when, if I should but seven years lie buried under the ground, and then arise and come thither again, I should not fail to find some therein that would bid me get out of doors, and tell me it were none of mine. What cause have I then to like such an house as would so soon forget his master?'

So her persuasions moved him but a little.

Not long after came there to him the Lord Chancellor, the Dukes of Norfolk and Suffolk with Master Secretary and certain other of the Privy Council, at two several times, by all policies possible procuring* him, either precisely to confess the Supremacy, or precisely to deny it. Whereunto, as appeareth by his examinations in the said great book,† they could never bring him.

Sir Richard Rich Lays a Trap

Shortly hereupon, Master Rich, afterwards Lord Rich, then newly made the King's Solicitor, Sir Richard Southwell, and one Master Palmer, servant to the Secretary, were sent to Sir Thomas More into the Tower to fetch away his books from him. And while Sir Richard Southwell and Master Palmer were busy in the trussing up of his books, Master Rich, pretending friendly talk with him, among other things, of a set course, as it seemed, said thus unto him:

'Forasmuch as it is well known, Master More, that you are a man both wise and well learned as well in the laws of the realm as otherwise, I pray you therefore, sir, let me be so bold as of good will to put unto you this case. Admit there were, sir,' quoth he, 'an act of Parliament that all the realm should take me for king. Would not you, Master More, take me for king?'

'Yes, sir,' quoth Sir Thomas More, 'that would I.'

'I put the case further,' quoth Master Rich, 'that there were an act of Parliament that all the realm should take me for Pope. Would not you then, Master More, take me for Pope?'

'For answer, sir,' quoth Sir Thomas More, 'to your first case, the Parliament may well, Master Rich, meddle with the state of temporal princes. But to make answer to your other cause, I will put this case – suppose the Parliament would make a law that God should not be God. Would you then, Master Rich, say that God were not God?'

'No, sir,' quoth he, 'that would I not, since no Parliament may make any such law.'

* urging. † see later p122.

38. *Lord Rich*

'No more', said Sir Thomas More, as Master Rich reported him, 'could the Parliament make the King Supreme Head of the Church.'

Upon whose only report was Sir Thomas More indicted for treason upon the statute whereby it was made treason to deny the King to be Supreme Head of the Church. Into which indictment were put these heinous words – 'maliciously, traitorously, and diabolically'.

The Trial – Rich's Perjury

When Sir Thomas More was brought from the Tower to Westminster Hall to answer the indictment, and at the King's Bench bar before the judges thereupon arraigned, he openly told them that he would upon that indictment have abidden* in law, but that he thereby should have been driven to confess of himself the matter indeed, that was the denial of the King's Supremacy. Which he protested was untrue. Wherefore he thereto pleaded not guilty; and so reserved unto himself advantage to be taken of the body of the matter, after verdict, to avoid that indictment. And moreover added that if those only odious terms, 'maliciously, traitorously, and diabolically' were put out of the indictment he saw therein nothing justly to charge him.

And for proof to the jury that Sir Thomas More was guilty of this treason, Master Rich was called forth to give evidence unto them upon his oath, as he did. Against whom thus sworn, Sir Thomas More began in this wise to say, 'If I were a man, my lords, that did not regard an oath, I needed not, as it is well known, in this place, at this time, nor in this case, to stand here as an accused person. And if this oath of yours, Master Rich, be true, then pray I that I never see God in the face, which I would not say, were it otherwise to win the whole world.' Then recited he to the court the discourse of all their communication in the Tower, according to the truth, and said, 'In good faith, Master Rich, I am sorrier for your perjury than for my own peril. And you shall understand that neither I, nor no man else to my knowledge, ever took you to be a man of such credit as in any matter of importance I, or any other, would at any time vouchsafe to communicate with you. And I, as you know, of no small while have been acquainted with you and your conversation, who have known you from your youth hitherto, for we have long dwelled in one parish together, where, as yourself can tell (I am sorry you compel me to say) you were esteemed very light of your tongue, a great dicer, and of no commendable fame. And so in your house at the Temple, where hath been your chief bringing up, were you likewise accounted.

* abided.

'Can it therefore seem likely unto your honourable lordships that I would, in so weighty a cause, so unadvisedly overshoot myself as to trust Master Rich, a man of me always reputed for one of so little truth, as your lordships have heard, so far above my sovereign lord the King or any of his noble Councillors, that I would unto him utter the secrets of my conscience touching the King's Supremacy, the special point and only mark at my hands so long sought for? A thing which I never did, nor never would, after the statute thereof made, reveal either to the King's highness himself or to any of his honourable Councillors; as it is not unknown to your honours, at sundry several times sent from his grace's own person unto the Tower unto me for none other purpose. Can this in your judgments, my lords, seem likely to be true? And yet, if I had so done indeed, my lords, as Master Rich hath sworn, seeing it was spoken but in familiar secret talk, nothing affirming, and only putting of cases, without other displeasant circumstances, it cannot justly be taken to be spoken maliciously, and where there is no malice, there can be no offence. And over this I can never think, my lords, that so many worthy bishops, so many honourable personages and so many other worshipful, virtuous, wise and well learned men as at the making of that law were in Parliament assembled, ever meant to have any man punished by death in whom there could be found no malice, taking "malitia" for "malevolentia". For if "malitia" be generally taken for "sin", no man is there then that can thereof excuse himself. *Quia si dixerimus quod peccatum non habemus, nosmet ipsos seducimus, et veritas in nobis non est.** And only this word "maliciously" is in the statute material, as this term "forcible" is in the statute of forcible entries, by which statute, if a man enter peaceably, and put not his adversary out forcibly, it is no offence. But if he put him out forcibly, then by that statute it is an offence, and so shall he be punished by this term "forcibly".

'Besides this, the manifold goodness of the King's highness himself, that hath been so many ways my singular good lord and gracious sovereign, that hath so dearly loved and trusted me, even at my very first coming into his noble service with the dignity of his honourable Privy Council vouchsafing to admit me, and to offices of great credit and worship most liberally advanced me. And finally with that weighty room of his grace's high Chancellor (the like whereof he never did to temporal man before), next to his own royal person the highest officer in this noble realm, so far above my merits or qualities able and meet

* 1 John i. 8: 'If we say that we have no sin, we deceive ourselves, and the truth is not in us.'

therefore, of his incomparable benignity honoured and exalted me, by the space of twenty years and more showing his continual favour towards me. And (until at mine own poor suit, it pleased his highness, giving me licence with his majesty's favour, to bestow the residue of my life for the provision of my soul in the service of God, of his especial goodness thereof to discharge and unburden me) most benignly heaped honours continually more and more upon me. All this his highness's goodness, I say, so long thus bountifully extended towards me, were in my mind, my lords, matter sufficient to convince this slanderous surmise by this man so wrongfully imagined against me.'

Master Rich, seeing himself so disproved, and his credit so foul defaced, caused Sir Richard Southwell and Master Palmer, that at the time of their communication were in the chamber, to be sworn what words had passed between them. Whereupon Master Palmer upon his deposition, said that he was so busy about the trussing up of Sir Thomas More's books in a sack, that he took no heed of their talk. Sir Richard Southwell likewise, upon his deposition, said that because he was appointed only to look unto the conveyance of his books, he gave no ear unto them.

After this were there many other reasons, not now to my remembrance, by Sir Thomas More in his own defence alleged, to the discredit of Master Rich's aforesaid evidence, and proof of the clearness of his own conscience. All which notwithstanding, the jury found him guilty. And incontinent upon their verdict, the Lord Chancellor, for that matter chief commissioner, beginning to proceed in judgment against him, Sir Thomas More said to him, 'My lord, when I was toward the law, the manner in such case was to ask the prisoner before judgment, why judgment should not be given against him.' Whereupon the Chancellor, staying his judgment, wherein he had partly proceeded, demanded of him what he was able to say to the contrary. Who then in this sort most humbly made answer:

'Forasmuch as, my lord,' quoth he, 'this indictment is grounded upon an act of Parliament directly repugnant to the laws of God and his holy Church, the supreme government of which or of any part whereof may no temporal prince presume by any law to take upon him, as rightfully belonging to the see of Rome, a spiritual pre-eminence by the mouth of our Saviour himself, personally present upon the earth, only to St Peter and his successors, bishops of the same see, by special prerogative granted, it is therefore in law amongst Christian men insufficient to charge any Christian man.' And for proof thereof, like as, among divers other reasons and authorities, he declared that this realm, being but one member and small part of the Church, might not make a

39. *Religious Conflict*

particular law disagreeable with the general law of Christ's universal Catholic Church, no more than the city of London, being but one poor member in respect of the whole realm, might make a law against an act of Parliament to bind the whole realm. So farther showed he that it was contrary both to the laws and statutes of our own land yet unrepealed, as they might evidently perceive in Magna Carta, *Quod Anglicana ecclesia libera sit, et habeat jura sua integra et libertates suas illaesas.** And also

* That the English Church shall be free, and shall have its rights undiminished and its liberties unimpaired.

contrary to that sacred oath which the King's highness himself and every other Christian prince always with great solemnity received at their coronations; alleging moreover that no more might this realm of England refuse obedience to the see of Rome than might a child refuse obedience to his own natural father. For as St Paul said to the Corinthians, 'I have regenerated you, my children in Christ.' So might St Gregory, Pope of Rome, of whom by St Augustine, his messenger, we first received the Christian faith, of us Englishmen truly say, 'You are my children, because I have given to you everlasting salvation, a far higher and better inheritance than any carnal father can leave to his child, and by regeneration made you my spiritual children in Christ.'

Then was it by the Lord Chancellor thereunto answered that seeing all the bishops, universities and best learned of this realm had to this act agreed, it was much marvelled that he alone against them all would so stiffly stick thereat, and so vehemently argue there against.

To that Sir Thomas More replied, saying, 'If the number of bishops and universities be so material as your lordship seemeth to take it, then see I little cause, my lord, why that thing in my conscience should make any change. For I nothing doubt but that, though not in this realm yet in Christendom about, of these well learned bishops and virtuous men that are yet alive, they be not the fewer part that be of my mind therein. But if I should speak of those which already be dead, of whom many be now holy saints in heaven, I am very sure it is the far greater part of them that, all the while they lived, thought in this case that way that I think now. And therefore am I not bound, my lord, to conform my conscience to the Council of one realm against the General Council of Christendom.'

Now when Sir Thomas More, for the voiding* of the indictment, had taken as many exceptions as he thought meet, and many more reasons than I can now remember alleged, the Lord Chancellor, loath to have the burden of that judgment wholly to depend on himself, there openly asked advice of the Lord FitzJames, then Lord Chief Justice of the King's Bench and joined in commission with him, whether this indictment were sufficient or not. Who, like a wise man, answered, 'My lords all, by St Julian' (that was ever his oath) 'I must needs confess that if the act of Parliament be not unlawful, then is not the indictment in my conscience insufficient.'

Whereupon the Lord Chancellor said to the rest of the lords, 'Lo, my lords, you hear what my Lord Chief Justice saith,' and so immediately gave he judgment against him.

* answering.

After which ended, the commissioners yet further courteously offered him, if he had anything else to allege for his defence, to grant him favourable audience. Who answered, 'More have I not to say, my lords, but that like the blessed apostle St Paul, as we read in the Acts of the Apostles, was present and consented to the death of St Stephen, and kept their clothes that stoned him to death, and yet be they now both twain holy saints in heaven, and shall continue there friends for ever, so I verily trust and shall therefore right heartily pray, that though your lordships have now here in earth been judges to my condemnation, we may yet hereafter in heaven merrily all meet together, to our everlasting salvation.'

This much touching Sir Thomas More's arraignment, being not thereat present myself, have I by credible report, partly of the right worshipful Sir Anthony St Leger, knight, and partly of Richard Heywood and John Webbe, gentlemen, with others of good credit, at the hearing thereof present themselves, as far as my poor wit and memory would serve me, here truly rehearsed unto you.

Now, after this arraignment, departed he from the bar to the Tower again, led by Sir William Kingston, a tall, strong and comely knight, Constable of the Tower, and his very dear friend. Who, when he had brought him from Westminster to the Old Swan towards the Tower, there with an heavy heart, the tears running down by his cheeks, bade him farewell. Sir Thomas More, seeing him so sorrowful, comforted him with as good words as he could, saying, 'Good Master Kingston, trouble not yourself, but be of good cheer; for I will pray for you, and my good lady your wife, that we may meet in heaven together where we shall be merry for ever and ever.'

Soon after, Sir William Kingston, talking with me of Sir Thomas More, said, 'In good faith, Master Roper, I was ashamed of myself, that, at my departing from your father, I found my heart so feeble, and his so strong, that he was fain to comfort me, which should rather have comforted him.'

More's Favourite Daughter, Margaret

When Sir Thomas More came from Westminster to the Towerward again, his daughter, my wife, desirous to see her father, whom she thought she should never see in this world after, and also to have his final blessing, gave attendance about the Tower wharf, where she knew he would pass by, before he could enter into the Tower, there tarrying for his coming home. As soon as she saw him, after his blessing on her knees reverently received, she hasting towards him, and without consideration or care of herself, pressing in among the middest of the

40. *London, with Old St Paul's*

throng and company of the guard that with halberds and bills went round about him, hastily ran to him, and there openly, in the sight of all, embraced him, took him about the neck and kissed him. Who, well liking her most natural and dear daughterly affection towards him, gave her his fatherly blessing and many godly words of comfort besides. From whom after she was departed, she, not satisfied with the former sight of him, and like one that had forgotten herself, being all ravished with the entire love of her dear father, having respect neither to herself nor to the press of the people and multitude that were there about him, suddenly turned back again, ran to him as before, took him about the neck, and divers times together most lovingly kissed him, and at last, with a full heavy heart, was fain to depart from him. The beholding whereof was to many of them that were present thereat so lamentable that it made them for very sorrow thereof to mourn and weep.

So remained Sir Thomas More in the Tower more than a seven-night after his judgment. From thence, the day before he suffered, he sent his shirt of hair (not willing to have it seen) to my wife, his dearly beloved daughter, and a letter written with a coal, contained in the foresaid book of his works, plainly expressing the fervent desire he had to suffer on the morrow, in these words following:

41. *The Tower, London Bridge, Southwark*

'I cumber you, good Margaret, much, but I would be sorry if it should be any longer than tomorrow, for tomorrow is St Thomas's even, and the utas* of St Peter. And therefore tomorrow long I to go to God; it were a day very meet and convenient for me . . . I never liked your manner towards me better than when you kissed me last. For I like when daughterly love and dear charity have no leisure to look to worldly courtesy.'

* octave.

Execution

And so upon the next morrow, being Tuesday, St Thomas's eve, and the utas of St Peter, in the year of our Lord one thousand five hundred thirty and five (according as he in his letter the day before had wished) early in the morning came to him Sir Thomas Pope, his singular friend, on message from the King and his Council, that he should before nine of the clock the same morning suffer death, and that therefore forthwith he should prepare himself thereto.

'Master Pope,' quoth he, 'for your good tidings I most heartily thank you. I have been always much bounden to the King's highness for the benefits and honours that he hath still from time to time most bountifully heaped upon me. And yet more bound am I to his grace for putting me into this place, where I have had convenient time and space to have remembrance of my end. And so help me, God, most of all, Master Pope, am I bound to his highness that it pleaseth him so shortly to rid me out of the miseries of this wretched world. And therefore will I not fail earnestly to pray for his grace, both here and also in another world.'

'The King's pleasure is further', quoth Master Pope, 'that at your execution you shall not use many words.'

'Master Pope,' quoth he, 'you do well to give me warning of his grace's pleasure, for otherwise I had purposed at that time somewhat to have spoken; but of no matter wherewith his grace, or any other, should have cause to be offended. Nevertheless, whatsoever I intended I am ready obediently to conform myself to his grace's commandments. And I beseech you, good Master Pope, to be a mean unto his highness that my daughter Margaret may be at my burial.'

'The King is content already', quoth Master Pope, 'that your wife, children and other your friends shall have liberty to be present thereat.'

'O how much beholden then', said Sir Thomas More, 'am I to his grace that unto my poor burial vouchsafeth to have so gracious consideration.'

Wherewithal Master Pope, taking his leave of him, could not refrain from weeping. Which Sir Thomas More perceiving, comforted him in this wise, 'Quiet yourself, good Master Pope, and be not discomforted, for I trust that we shall, once in heaven, see each other merrily, where we shall be sure to live and love together, in joyful bliss eternally.'

Upon whose departure, Sir Thomas More, as one that had been invited to some solemn feast, changed himself into his best apparel, which Master Lieutenant espying, advised him to put it off, saying that he that should have it was but a javel.*

* low fellow.

'What, Master Lieutenant,' quoth he, 'shall I account him a javel that shall do me this day so singular a benefit? Nay, I assure you, were it cloth of gold, I would account it well bestowed on him, as St Cyprian did, who gave his executioner thirty pieces of gold.' And albeit at length through Master Lieutenant's importunate persuasion he altered his apparel, yet after the example of St Cyprian, did he, of that little money that was left him, send one angel of gold to his executioner.

And so was he by Master Lieutenant brought out of the Tower, and from thence led towards the place of execution. Where, going up the scaffold, which was so weak that it was ready to fall, he said merrily to Master Lieutenant, 'I pray you, Master Lieutenant, see me safe up, and for my coming down let me shift for myself.'

Then desired he all the people thereabout to pray for him, and to bear witness with him that he should now suffer death in and for the faith of the holy Catholic Church. Which done, he knelt down, and after his prayers said, turned to the executioner and with a cheerful countenance spake thus to him: 'Pluck up thy spirits, man, and be not afraid to do thine office; my neck is very short; take heed therefore thou strike not awry, for saving of thine honesty.'

So passed Sir Thomas More out of this world to God, upon the very same day in which himself had most desired.

Soon after whose death came intelligence thereof to the Emperor Charles. Whereupon he sent for Sir Thomas Elyot, our English Ambassador, and said unto him: 'My Lord ambassador, we understand that the King, your master, hath put his faithful servant and grave wise councillor, Sir Thomas More, to death.' Whereunto Sir Thomas Elyot answered that he understood nothing thereof. 'Well,' said the Emperor, 'it is too true. And this will we say, that if we had been master of such a servant, of whose doings our self have had these many years no small experience, we would rather have lost the best city of our dominions than have lost such a worthy councillor.' Which matter was by the same Sir Thomas Elyot to myself, to my wife, to Master Clement and his wife, to Master John Heywood and his wife, and unto divers other his friends accordingly reported.

Finis *Deo gratias*

A Selection of More's Letters

1. To Joyce Lee

The first of More's English letters to come down to us is that with which he sent his translation of the Life of Pico della Mirandola. *The work itself illustrates More's interest in the Renaissance humanists, of whom he was a leading English figure himself. This letter of 1505 shows how much it was the religious side of humanism, Christian Humanism, that appealed to him. The letter was addressed to a nun of the order of Poor Clares, sister of Archbishop Lee of York.*

Unto his right entirely beloved sister in Christ, Joyce Lee, Thomas More greeting in our Lord.

It is and of long time hath been, my well beloved sister, a custom in the beginning of the New Year friends to send between presents of gifts as the witnesses of their love and friendship. And also signifying that they desire each to other that year a good continuance and prosperous end of

42. *Pica della Mirandola*

that lucky beginning. But commonly all those presents that are used customably, all in this manner between friends to be sent, be such things as pertain only unto the body – either to be fed, or to be clad, or some otherwise delighted. By which it seemeth that their friendship is but fleshly and stretcheth in manner to the body only. But forasmuch as the love and amity of Christian folk should be rather ghostly friendship than bodily, sith [since] that all faithful people are rather spiritual than carnal. For, as the apostle saith, we be not now in flesh but in spirit, if Christ abide in us – I therefore, mine heartily beloved sister, in good luck of this New Year have sent you such a present as may bear witness of my tender love and zeal to the happy continuance and gracious increase of virtue in your soul. And whereas the gifts of other folk declare that they wisheth their friends to be worldly fortunate, mine testifieth that I desire to have you godly prosperous . . .

2. To Wolsey

The following portion of a letter to Wolsey, from Woking, 5 July 1519, shows More in intimate attendance upon Henry VIII, receiving the Cardinal's letters about affairs, reading them to the King, and returning his reply.

. . . Sir, if it like your grace, at my return when I spake with the King his grace was very joyful that, notwithstanding your so continual labours in his matters (in which, he said, ye have many more than appear to them that see you but at Westminster or with the Council) your grace is so well in health, as he heareth by divers. And he saith that ye may thank his counsel thereof, by which ye leave the often taking of medicines that ye were wont to use. And while ye so do, he saith, ye shall not fail of health, which our Lord long preserve.

3. To Wolsey

Next day More was writing to Wolsey again on behalf of the King concerning relations with King Charles, shortly to become the Emperor Charles V. Three days later again we see Henry in a more personal light, concerning himself with the marriage of his Yorkist cousin, Henry Courtenay, Earl of Devon, who subsequently married Lord Mountjoy's daughter and was executed some nineteen years later for his proximity to the throne. More reports to Wolsey from Woking, 9 July 1519:

43. *The Emperor Charles V*

And as touching the overture made by my Lord of Chièvres* for the marriage of my Lord of Devonshire, the King is well content and, as me seemeth, very glad of the motion. Wherein he requireth your grace that it may like you to call my Lord of Devonshire to your grace and to advise him secretly to forbear any further treaty of marriage with my Lord Mountjoy. For a while staying the matter, not casting it off; showing him that there is a far better offer made him, of which the King would that he should not know the speciality before he speak with his grace.

* Charles V's Flemish minister.

As touching the demeanour of the Cardinal Sedunense [of Sion], concerning the trust that the King's grace did put in him – his grace commanded me to show your grace that he mistrusted the same himself before, and that he so showed your grace at Richmond. And though he be not glad of the Cardinal's dealing, yet is he glad, he saith, that your grace may see that he foresaw it. Whereby he thinketh your grace will the better trust his conjecture hereafter . . .

4. To Wolsey

Most of More's letters are in Latin. It is interesting that those to Wolsey are in English – evidently the Cardinal's Latin had grown rusty with the years in office and the burden of affairs. He was a prodigious worker; Henry appreciated that. But in these letters of intimate attendance upon the King, with More writing the most confidential communications to the Cardinal, we see that Henry already took full share in the business of state, great and small, and had the final voice in decisions of policy. More's letters from Court offer an invaluable close-up of the King in action.

Wolsey addressed his letters to More to be read to Henry, who thereupon instructed More what to reply. In the following letter, from Newhall 21 September 1522, we see how closely associated More was with affairs of state, the confidence reposed in him by King and Cardinal, and the familiar access he had in the course of his duties.

. . . Which things with diligence I presented forthwith unto the King's grace the same morning. And to the intent that his grace should the more perfectly perceive what weighty things they were that your grace had sent unto him, and what diligence was requisite in the expediting of the same, I read unto his grace the letters which it liked your grace to write to me.

In which it much liked his grace that your grace so well allowed and approved his opinion concerning the overtures made by the French King unto the Emperor.* After your grace's said letter read, when he saw of your grace's own hand that I should diligently solicit the expedition of those other things – forasmuch as your grace intended and gladly would dispatch the premises this present Sunday – his grace laughed and said: 'Nay, by my soul, that will not be; for this is my removing day soon at New Hall. I will read the remnant at night.'

* Diplomatic sparring prior to the outbreak of war between them; in which Henry went over to the Emperor's side against France, the popular course to take.

Whereupon, after that his grace was come home hither and had dined, being six of the clock in the night, I offered myself again to his grace in his own chamber. At which time he was content to sign the letters to the Emperor and the other letters for the expedition of the gentleman of Spruce,* putting over all the remnant till this day in the morning.

Whereupon, at my parting from his grace yesternight, I received from your grace a letter addressed unto his. With which I forthwith returned unto his grace in the Queen's chamber.† Where his grace read openly my Lord Admiral's‡ letter to the Queen; which marvellously rejoiced in the good news, and specially in that that the French King should be now toward a tutor and his realm to have a governor.

In the communication whereof, which lasted about one hour, the King's grace said that he trusted in God to be their governor himself; and that they should by this means make a way for him, as King Richard did for his father. I pray God, if it be good for his grace and for this realm, that then it may prove so; and else, in the stead thereof, I pray God send his grace an honourable and profitable peace.

This day in the morning I read unto his grace as well the instructions most politicly and most prudently devised by your grace, and thereto most eloquently expressed, as all the letters of Mr Secretary sent unto your grace. To whom as well for your speedy advertisement in the one, as for your great labour and pain taken in the other, his grace giveth his most hearty thanks . . .

Forasmuch as the King's grace hath not yet written of his own hand the minute to the Emperor, which I delivered his grace in this morning, therefore I suppose that this letter, written this present Sunday the XXI day of September in the night, can not be delivered to the post till tomorrow about ——, as knoweth our Lord, who long preserve your grace in honour and health.

5. To Wolsey

More's next letter to Wolsey, from Easthampstead 26 August 1523, gave Henry's forthright declaration against any licence to the Emperor's subjects to trade with France during the continuance of the war, 'the commodities of France having vent and utterance, the enemy thereby better furnished of money should be the more able the longer to maintain the war.' In the second subject recurs Henry's interest in the defence of the Catholic faith, upon

* An envoy from Prussia. † Henry's first Queen, Catherine of Aragon.
‡ The Earl of Surrey, later Duke of Norfolk.

44. *Field of Cloth of Gold*

which he wrote his book against Luther, with some help from More, and for which the Pope awarded Henry the title 'Defender of the Faith', which he retained in spite of the subsequent break with Rome.

. . . It may further like your good grace to be advertised that one Thomas Murner, a friar of St Francis' Order, which wrote a book against Luther in defence of the King's book, was out of Almain [Germany] sent into England by the mean of a simple person: an Almain [German] naming himself servant unto the King's grace. And

affirming unto Murner that the King had given him in charge to desire Murner to come over to him into England. And by the occasion thereof he is come over and hath now been here a good while.

Wherefore the King's grace – pitying that he was so deceived and having tender respect to the good zeal that he beareth toward the Faith, and his good heart and mind toward his highness – requireth your grace that it may like you to cause him have in reward £100. And that he may return home, where his presence is very necessary. For he is one of the chief stays against the faction of Luther in that part, against whom he hath written many books in the Almain tongue. And now, sith his coming hither, he hath translated into Latin the book that he before

45. *Martin Luther*

ASSERTIO
septem Sacramentorum ad-
uersus Martin. Lu-
therum, ædita ab
inuictissimo
Angliæ
&
Franciæ rege, & do. Hyberniæ Hē-
rico eius nominis octauo.

46. *Henry VIII's Reply to Luther*

made in Almain in defence of the King's book. He is doctor of divinity, and of both laws [civil and canon law], and a man for writing and preaching of great estimation in his country . . .

Furthermore, it may like your good grace to understand that, at the contemplation of your grace's letters, the King's highness is graciously content that – beside the £100 for my fee for the office of the Speaker of this Parliament, to be taken at the Receipt of his Exchequer – I shall have one other £100 out of his coffers, by the hands of the Treasurer of his Chamber. Wherefore in most humble wise I beseech your good grace that, as your gracious favour hath obtained it for me, so it may like the same to write to Mr Wyatt* that he may deliver it to such as I shall send for it . . .

6. To Wolsey

With England at war with France the Scots, as the allies of France, usually attacked over the Border. Henry's sister, Margaret, had been married to James IV of Scotland – which had not prevented him from invading England in Henry's first French war, when James was overthrown and killed at Flodden in 1513. Ten years later, in Henry's second French war, Queen Margaret was at the head of the English faction in Scotland. More was writing to Wolsey, on behalf of Henry only a few days after the previous letter, from Woking 1 September 1523.

It may like your good grace to be advertised that I have received your grace's letters directed to myself, dated the last day of August, with the letters of my Lord Admiral to your grace sent in post. And copies of letters sent between the Queen of Scots and his lordship, concerning the matters and affairs of Scotland; with the prudent answers of your grace to my said Lord in your own name as in the name of the King's highness to the said Queen of Scots. All which letters and copies I have distinctly read unto his grace. Who hath in the reading thereof substantially considered as well the Queen his sister's letter, with the letters againward devised and sent by my Lord Admiral to her and his letters of advertisement to your grace, as your most politic devices and answers unto all the same. Among which the letter which your grace devised, in the name of his highness to the Queen his sister, his grace so well liked that I never saw him like thing better. And, as help me God, in my poor fantasy not causeless; for it is, for the quantity, one of the best made

* Sir Henry Wyatt, Treasurer of the King's Chamber.

letters for words, matter, sentence, and couching that ever I read in my life.

His highness, in your grace's letter directed to my Lord Admiral, marked and well liked that your grace touched my said Lord and my Lord Dacre, in that their opinions had been to the let [hindrance] of the great road. Which, if it had been ere this time made into Scotland – as by your prudent advice it had, if their opinions with others had not been to the contrary – it should, as by the Queen's letter appeareth, have been the occasion of some great and good effect . . .

In the reading and advising of all which things his highness said that he perceived well what labour, study, pain and travail your grace had taken in the device and penning of so many, so great things, so high – well dispatched in so brief time, when the only reading thereof held him above two hours. His highness therefore commanded me to write unto your grace that – for your labour, travail, study, pain and diligence – he giveth your grace his most hearty, and not more hearty than highly well-deserved, thanks.

7. To Wolsey

Two days later More is writing to Wolsey, from Woking 3 September 1523, forwarding the congratulatory letter Henry had signed to the Doge of Venice on making peace with the Emperor. More continues:

. . . I read also to his highness your said letters written to me, which his highness very gladly heard and, in the reading, said that your grace was worthy more thanks than he could give you. And as touching the venison which he sent your grace, he was very glad that it liked your grace so well, and would that it had been much better . . .

8. To Wolsey

Meanwhile Wolsey had commended More for his good service, as we find from More's letter two days later from Woking, 5 September. We have seen that More himself was on such good terms with the almighty Cardinal as to put forward his own praise of Wolsey's diplomatic dispatches. He continues:

. . . Where it liketh your good grace so thankfully to accept my poor devoir [duty] in doing right small part of my bounden duty, ye show your accustomed goodness, and bind me that that in my service lacketh in my poor prayer to supply.

47. *Cardinal Wolsey*

48. *More's Youngest Daughter*

9. To Wolsey

A letter to Wolsey next year, from Hertford 29 November 1524, gives a further lively close-up of Henry VIII's alert attention to affairs.

It may like your good grace to be advertised that yesternight, at my coming unto the King's grace's presence, after that I had made your grace's recommendations and his highness showed himself very greatly glad and joyful of your grace's health – As I was about to declare further to his grace what letters I had brought, his highness, perceiving letters in my hand, prevented me ere I could begin, and said: 'Ha! ye have letters now by John Joachim* and, I trow, some resolution what they will do.'

'Nay, verily, sir,' quoth I, 'my lord hath yet no word by John Joachim, nor John Joachim – as far as my lord knew – had yet no word himself this day in the morning when I departed from his grace.'

'No had?' quoth he, 'I much marvel thereof; for John Joachim had a servant come to him two days ago.'

'Sir,' quoth I, 'if it like your grace, this morning my lord's grace had nothing heard thereof . . . Where, at my coming, he delivered me these other letters and advertisements sent unto him from Mr Pace.† Commanding me that, after your highness had seen them . . . he would show them to others of your grace's Council – as also to John Joachim, for the contents be such as will do him little pleasure.'

'Mary,' quoth his grace, 'I am well a-paid thereof.'

And so he fell in merrily to the reading of Master Pace and all the other abstracts and writings, whereof the contents as highly contented him as any tidings that I have seen come to him . . . And forthwith he declared the news and every material point, which upon the reading his grace well noted unto the Queen's grace and all others about him, who were marvellous glad to hear it. And the Queen's grace said that she was glad that the Spaniards had yet done somewhat in Italy, in recompense of their departure out of Provence . . .

10. To his wife, Alice

The following is the only letter from More to his wife that survives. It was written from the Court at Woodstock, 3 September 1529, upon his return from his embassy at Cambrai. The letter speaks for itself – More's charitable concern for his poor neighbours rather than his own losses from the fire that had consumed part of his house at Chelsea, with his barns full of corn after harvest.

Mistress Alice, in my most hearty wise I recommend me to you. And whereas I am informed by my son [-in-law] Heron of the loss of our barns and our neighbours' also with all the corn that was therein, albeit (saving God's pleasure) it were great pity of so much good corn lost – yet, sith it hath liked him to send us such a chance, we must and are

* Giovanni Gioachino Passano, a Genoese merchant, was employed in secret negotiations between France and England.
† Richard Pace, humanist scholar, was a leading diplomat, much employed on missions abroad.

bounden not only to be content but also to be glad of his visitation. He sent us all that we have lost and, since he hath by such a chance taken it away again, his pleasure be fulfilled. Let us never grudge thereat, but take in good worth and heartily thank him as well for adversity as for prosperity. And peradventure we have more cause to thank him for our loss than for our winning, for his wisdom better seeth what is good for us than we do ourselves.

Therefore, I pray you, be of good cheer and take all the household with you to church, and there thank God both for that he hath given us and for that he hath taken from us and for that he hath left us. Which, if it please him, he can increase when he will and if it please him to leave us yet less, at his pleasure be it.

I pray you to make some good ensearch what my poor neighbours have lost and bid them take no thought therefore. For and [if] I should not leave myself a spoon, there shall no poor neighbour of mine bear no loss by any chance happened in my house. I pray you be with my children and your household merry in God, and devise somewhat with your friends what way were best to take for provision to be made for corn for our household, and for seed this year coming, if ye think it good that we keep the ground still in our hands. Yet I think it were not best suddenly thus to leave it all up and to put away our folk of our farm, till we have somewhat advised us thereon. Howbeit, if we have more now than ye shall need and which can get them other masters, ye may then discharge us of them. But I would not that any man were suddenly sent away, he wot [knew] ne'er whither.

At my coming hither I perceived none other but that I should tarry still with the King's grace. But now I shall, I think, because of this chance get leave this next week to come home and see you. And then shall we further devise together upon all things what order shall be best to take.

11. To the 'Nun of Kent'

The question of Henry VIII's divorce from Queen Catherine hung over the country for years and produced a fearful problem – most of all for himself. It was a prime duty to ensure the succession to the throne with a legitimate male heir. Henry convinced himself that his marriage to his brother's widow was condemned by Scripture and unlawful, and was null. After years of waiting and negotiating with the Papacy for a declaration of nullity, at the first sign that Anne Boleyn was pregnant he married her, hoping for a son, and broke with Rome.

The marriage with Anne was unpopular with many. The notorious 'Nun of Kent' took it upon herself to campaign in the King's 'great matter'; her pretended visions and prophecies of ill encouraged opposition on a most sensitive personal concern for the King and a critical issue of state. The Nun's public campaign endangered various high ecclesiastics, and suspicion fell upon More for his communications with her. In the Act of Attainder against those challenging the succession, More's name was originally included, but was withdrawn at the wish of the Lords and upon his clearing himself. The following letter shows that More had advised the meddlesome woman for her own good, and had been careful not to commit himself – as the credulous Bishop Fisher had done. At her execution the Nun admitted that her visions had been all pretence, herself 'a poor wench without learning', puffed up by the praises of learned men – and, we should say, the itch for publicity.

More had written to her as follows.

Good Madam, and my right dearly beloved Sister in our Lord God.

. . . Good Madam, I doubt not but that you remember that in the beginning of my communication with you, I showed you that I neither was nor would be curious of any knowledge of other men's matters. And least of all of any matter of princes or of the realm. In case it so were that God had – as to many good folks before time he hath – revealed unto you such things, I said unto your ladyship that I was not only not desirous to hear of, but also would not hear of.

Now, Madam, I consider well that many folk desire to speak with you, which are not all peradventure of my mind in this point . . . And some might peradventure hap to talk of such things, as might peradventure after turn to much harm. As I think you have heard how the late Duke of Buckingham – moved with the fame of one that was reported for an holy monk – and had such talking with him as after was a great part of his destruction and disinheriting of his blood, and great slander and infamy of religion.*

It sufficeth me, good Madam, to put you in remembrance of such thing, as I nothing doubt your wisdom and the spirit of God shall keep you from talking with any persons – specially with lay persons – of any such manner things as pertain to princes' affairs, or the state of the realm. But only to commune and talk with any person, high and low, of such manner things as may to the soul be profitable for you to show and for them to know.

* Edward Stafford, Duke of Buckingham, had been betrayed by his foolish confessor, who prophesied that Henry VIII would have no male heir and that Buckingham would succeed him on the throne.

12. To Cromwell

So critical was the issue of the succession and the breach with Rome occasioned by it that More was henceforth in danger, for – though he kept silent on both issues – his opinions were known. He had resigned from being Lord Chancellor, Wolsey's successor, for he regarded the policy whose leading exponent was Thomas Cromwell, though supported by Parliament and accepted by the episcopate (except for Fisher), as contrary to his own beliefs and conscience.

Nevertheless, he had to explain himself to Cromwell regarding his contacts with the Nun of Kent. He wrote from his home at Chelsea – to which he had at length withdrawn from his many years at Court and in public life – shortly before the Nun's execution in April 1534, as follows.

Right Worshipful, after right hearty recommendation, so it is that I am informed that there is a bill put in against me, into the higher House before the Lords, concerning my communication with the Nun of Canterbury, and my writing unto her. Whereof I not a little marvel, the truth of the matter being such as God and I know it is, and as I have plainly declared unto you by my former letters. Wherein I found you then so good that I am now bold eftsoons [so soon] upon your goodness to desire you to show me that favour as that I might, the rather by your good means, have a copy of the bill.

Which seen, if I find any untrue surmise therein – as of likelihood there is – I may make mine humble suit unto the King's good grace and declare the truth: either to his grace, or by his grace's commandment wheresoever the matter shall require. I am so sure of my truth toward his grace that I cannot mistrust his gracious favour toward me, upon the truth known, nor the judgement of any honest man. Nor never shall there loss in this matter grieve me, being myself so innocent as God and I know me – whatsoever should happen to me therein, by the grace of Almighty God, who both bodily and ghostly preserve you.

13. To the King

On 5 March 1534 More wrote to the King, repeating what he had written to Cromwell 'in this matter of the wicked woman of Canterbury', and continuing:

Wherefore, most gracious sovereign, I neither will, nor well it can become me, with your highness to reason and argue the matter; but in my most humble manner, prostrate at your gracious feet, I only beseech your majesty, with your own high prudence and your accustomed goodness, consider and weigh the matter. And then, if in your so doing, your own virtuous mind shall give you that – notwithstanding the manifold excellent goodness that your gracious highness hath by so many manner ways used unto me – I be a wretch of such a monstrous ingratitude as could, with any of them all or any other person living, digress from my bounden duty of allegiance toward your good grace. Then desire I not further favour at your gracious hand than the loss of all that ever I may lose in this world – goods, lands, and liberty, and finally my life with all. Whereof the keeping of any part unto myself could never do me pennyworth of pleasure. But only should then my recomfort be that – after my short life and your long (which, with continual prosperity to God's pleasure, our Lord for his mercy send you) I should once meet with your grace again in heaven, and there be merry with you. Where, among mine other pleasures, this should yet be one, that your grace should surely see there then, that – howsoever you take me – I am your true bedeman [supplicator] now and ever have been, and will be till I die, howsoever your pleasure be to do by me . . .

14. To Cromwell

More's appeal to Henry did him no good in that quarter: his personal devotion to the King, who had been so good to him, was not the point; nor was length of life (More was a year older than Henry at their deaths); nor the prospect of being merry, as in old days at Court, but in heaven. Henry was sick and tired of argumentation about the Divorce; he was himself caught in a vice between two stubborn, obstinate women, Catherine and Anne; in the struggle his naive and passionate love for the latter turned sour. But he had made his decision, supported by Parliament and the Church in England, both of which understood the dire necessity he was under of providing for the succession, over which indeed he had hesitated and delayed too long. (When he died he left a boy of nine to succeed him, who died in turn at sixteen.)

A secure and legitimate succession was a prime national need. Only a few fractious persons stood out – but one of them was the most distinguished man in the country, its most famous scholar and writer, the man whom the King had delighted to honour, to whom he had given the highest office in the country, the first layman to be Lord Chancellor.

Opposition now made Henry mad – the strain he had been under for so long hardened his character, and brought out the capricious cruelty he inherited from his Yorkist grandfather, Edward IV. There is no doubt that he regarded More's opposition, in his own appalling situation, as black

49. *Thomas Cromwell's Remembrances*

ingratitude and was determined to frame him, though Roper tells us that it was Queen Anne's nagging that drove Henry to the last step of taking More's life.

On the same day he wrote to the King, More addressed an immensely long letter to Cromwell, explaining his position and recounting his dealings with Henry over his marriage. Roper incorporates the important passage from this letter in which More had earlier warned Henry from stating too absolute a view of the Papal primacy in his book against Luther, in case he might find it awkward later on; Henry, bull-headed as usual, would take no notice. History is full of such ironies, of people reversing their positions, taken up with too much assurance.

On the excruciating question of the King's Divorce More writes to Cromwell:

. . . Sir, upon a time at my coming from beyond the sea, where I had been in the King's business, I repaired, as my duty was, unto the King's grace, being at that time at Hampton Court. At which time his highness, suddenly walking in the gallery, broke with me of his great matter. And showed me that it was now perceived that his marriage [i.e. to Catherine] was not only against the positive laws of the Church and the written law of God, but also in such wise against the law of nature that it could in no wise by the Church be dispensable.

Now so it was that, before my going over the sea, I had heard certain things moved against the Bull of the dispensation, concerning the words of the law Levitical and the law Deuteronomical to prove the prohibition to be *de iure divino* [of divine right]. But yet perceived I not at that time but that the greater hope of that matter stood in certain faults that were found in the Bull, whereby the Bull should by the law not be sufficient . . .

50. *Thomas Cromwell*

The first time that ever I heard that point moved – that it should be in such high degree against the law of nature – was the time in which . . . the King's grace showed it me himself; and laid the Bible open before me. And there read me the words that moved his highness, and divers other erudite persons, so to think; and asked me what myself thought thereon . . . I showed, as my duty was at his commandment, what thing I thought upon the words which I there read.

Whereupon his highness, accepting benignly my sudden unadvised answer, commanded me to commune further with Mr Fox,* now his grace's Almoner, and to read a book with him that then was in making for that matter . . . His highness, like a prudent and a virtuous prince, assembled at another time at Hampton Court a good number of very well learned men – at which time . . . there were (as was in so great a matter most likely to be) divers opinions among them. Howbeit, I never heard but that they agreed upon a certain form in which the book should be made. Which book was afterward at York Place [Whitehall], in my Lord Cardinal's chamber, read in the presence of divers bishops and many learned men. And they all thought that there appeared in the book good and reasonable causes that might well move the King's highness, being so virtuous a prince, to conceive in his mind a scruple against his marriage. Which, while he could not otherwise avoid, he did well and virtuously for the quieting of his conscience to sue and procure to have his doubt decided by judgement of the Church . . .

* Edward Fox, soon made Bishop of Hereford.

51. *Hampton Court*

15. To Margaret

More's next letter, written to his daughter Margaret from the Tower in April 1534, is that referred to by Roper as printed in More's Works. *Though very long, it gives such a vivid account of his examination before the Lords of the Council that we give most of it. The salient point is that More was prepared to swear to the succession, i.e. Queen Anne's daughter Elizabeth as heir, but would not take the oath abjuring Papal authority. Archbishop Cranmer, a kind and clever man, tried to save him by thinking of an argument which surprised More. Of the men who appeared that day it is sufficient witness of the time to record their fates: Cranmer, burned; Latimer, burned; More and Fisher, executed, as was Cromwell himself.*

When I was before the Lords at Lambeth I was the first that was called in . . . After the cause of my sending for declared unto me (whereof I somewhat marvelled in my mind, considering that they sent for no more temporal men but me*) I desired the sight of the oath, which they showed me under the great seal. Then desired I the sight of the Act of the Succession, which was delivered me in a printed roll. After which read secretly by myself, and the oath considered with the Act, I showed unto them that my purpose was not to put any fault either in the Act or any man that made it; or in the oath or any man that swore it; nor to condemn the conscience of any man.

* An aura of the clerical attached to the Lord Chancellorship, which, until More, had always been held by a cleric.

But as for myself in good faith my conscience so moved me in the matter that, though I would not deny to swear to the succession, yet unto the oath that there was offered me I could not swear without the jeoparding of my soul to perpetual damnation . . .

Unto this my Lord Chancellor said that they all were sorry to hear me say thus, and see me thus refuse the oath. And they said all that, on their faith, I was the very first that ever refused it: which would cause the King's highness to conceive great suspicion of me and great indignation toward me. And therewith they showed me the roll, and let me see the names of the Lords and the Commons which had sworn and subscribed their names already.

Which notwithstanding, when they saw that I refused to swear the same myself . . . I was in conclusion commanded to go down into the garden. And thereupon I tarried in the old burned chamber that looketh into the garden, and would not go down because of the heat. In that time I saw Master Doctor Latimer come into the garden, and there walked he with divers other doctors and chaplains of my Lord of Canterbury. And very merry I saw him, for he laughed and took one or twain about the neck so handsomely that, if they had been women, I would have went [i.e. thought] he had been waxen wanton . . .

52. *Bishop Latimer*

53. *Bishop Fisher*

What time my Lord of Rochester [Fisher] was called in before them, that can I not tell. But at night I heard that he had been before them, but where he remained that night and so forth till he was sent hither [the Tower], I never heard . . .

When they had played their pageant and were gone out of the place, then was I called in again. And then it was declared unto me what a number had sworn ever since I went aside – gladly, without any sticking. Wherein I laid no blame on no man, but for mine own self answered as before. Now, they somewhat laid unto me for obstinacy that . . . I would not declare any special part of that oath that grudged my conscience, and open the cause wherefore. For thereunto I had said to them that I feared the King's highness would take displeasure enough toward me for the only refusal of the oath. And that, if I should open and disclose the causes why, I should therewith but further exasperate his highness . . .

My Lord of Canterbury, taking hold upon that that I had said – that I condemned not the conscience of them that swore – said unto me that it appeared well that I did not take it for a very sure thing and a certain that I might not lawfully swear it, but rather as a thing uncertain and doubtful. But then, said my Lord, you know for a certainty and a thing without doubt that you be bound to obey your sovereign lord, your King. And therefore are ye bound to leave off the doubt of your unsure conscience in refusing the oath, and take the sure way in obeying of your prince, and swear it.*

Now all was it so that in mine own mind methought myself not concluded. Yet this argument seemed me suddenly so subtle, and

* Compare Dr Johnson's 'He is no wise man who will quit a certainty for an uncertainty'.

namely with such authority coming out of so noble a prelate's mouth, that I could again answer nothing thereto – but only that I thought myself I might not well do so. Because that in my conscience this was one of the cases in which I was bound that I should not obey my prince . . .

Then said my Lord of Westminster [i.e. the Abbot] that, howsoever the matter seemed unto mine own mind, I had cause to fear that mine own mind was erroneous – when I see the great Council of the realm [i.e. Parliament, Lords and Commons] determine of my mind the contrary. And that therefore I ought to change my conscience.

To that I answered that, if there were no more but myself upon my side, and the whole Parliament upon the other, I would be sore afraid to lean to mine own mind only against so many. But, on the other side, if it so be that in some things for which I refuse the oath, I have (as I think I have) upon my part as great a council, and a greater too, I am not then bound to change my conscience and conform it to the council of one realm against the general council of Christendom.

Upon this, Master Secretary [Cromwell], as he that tenderly favoureth me, said and swore a great oath that he had liever [rather] that his own only son (which is of truth a goodly young gentleman, and shall, I trust, come to much worship*) had lost his head than that I should thus have refused the oath. For surely the King's highness would now conceive a great suspicion against me, and think that the matter of the Nun of Canterbury was all contrived by my drift.

To which I said that the contrary was true and well known. And whatsoever should mishap me, it lay not in my power to help it without peril of my soul . . .

16. To Margaret

The previous letter contained further quibbling on More's part as to the character of the oath which he was willing to swear to. He made it clear that it would have to be drafted by himself. What he objected to was the abjuration of Papal authority, though he elsewhere states that he did not place it above that of a General Council. So it was for that 'foreign jurisdiction', as it was phrased, that More insisted on dying. It is plain from his last letters to Margaret Roper from the Tower that he desired martyrdom. He had his wish.

* It was the father, not the son, who lost his head; in subsequent regret for which Henry made Gregory Cromwell a peer. There was not much to him.

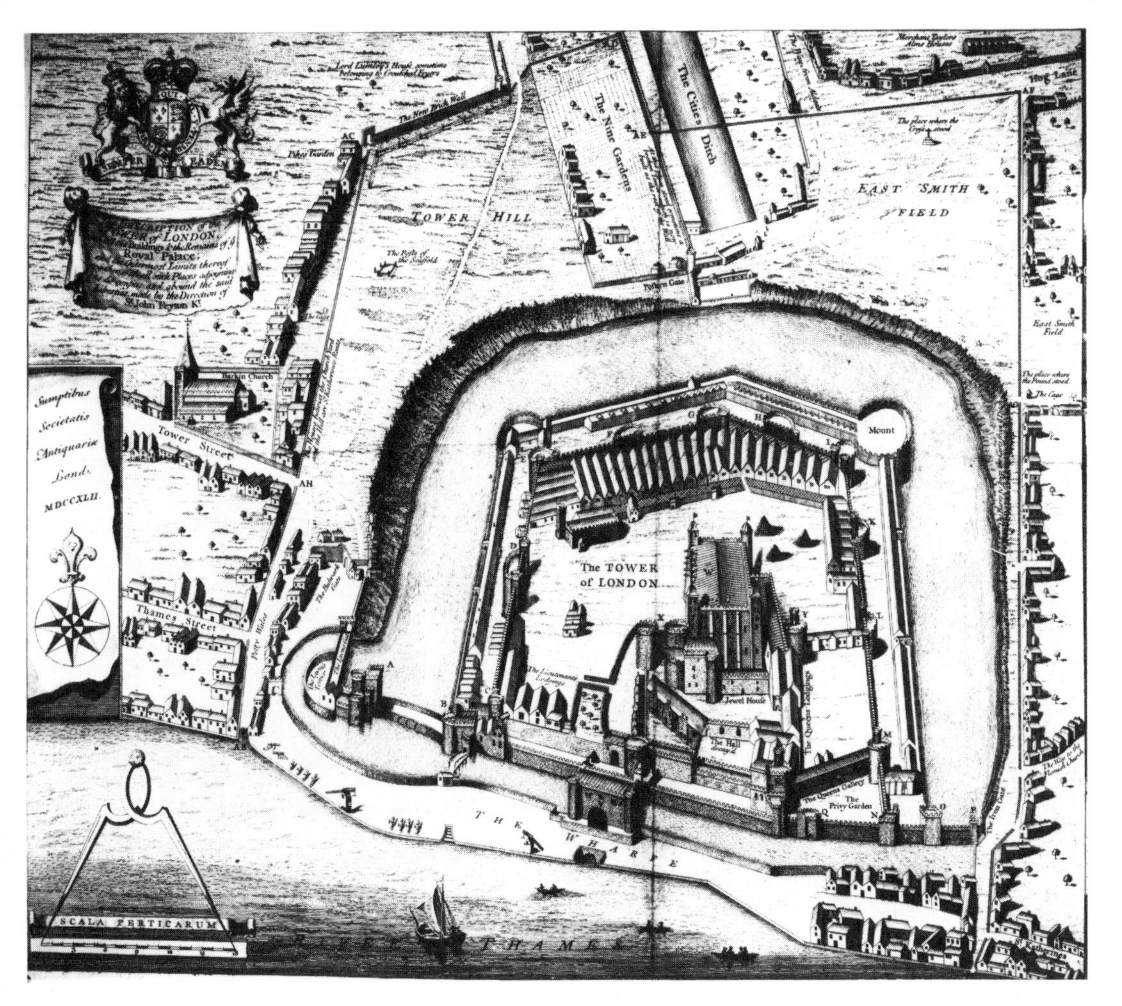

54. *The Tower of London*

Mine own good daughter, our Lord be thanked, I am in good health of body and in good quiet of mind; and of worldly things I desire no more than I have. I beseech him make you all merry in the hope of heaven. And such things as I somewhat longed to talk with you all, concerning the world to come, our Lord put them into your minds, as I trust he doth, and better too, by his holy spirit: who bless you and preserve you all.

Written with a coal by your tender loving father, who in his poor prayers forgetteth none of you all; nor your babes, nor your nurses, nor your good husbands, nor your good husbands' shrewd wives, nor your father's shrewd wife neither, nor our other friends. And thus fare you heartily well for lack of paper.

Thomas More, Knight.

Our Lord keep me continually true faithful and plain: to the contrary whereof I beseech him heartily never to suffer me live. For, as for long life (as I have often told thee, Meg), I neither look for, nor long for, but am well content to go if God call me hence tomorrow . . .

More was kept in the Tower for more than a year, until July 1535 in fact. Evidently the government did not wish to incur the ignominy of executing him. Nor could he be trapped into saying openly what he objected to in the oath which he refused to take. On that he kept to his policy of silence – not for nothing was he the ablest lawyer in the country.

His greatest fear was that he might be induced to relent by the persuasions of those whom he loved, particularly from his favourite daughter Margaret, who urged him at one point to give way and have a care of his family. This is the subject of a long letter of tender reproof to her and of self-justification.

He wrote, 'And now you see well, Margaret, that it is no obstinacy to leave the causes undeclared, while I could not declare them without peril. But now it is accounted great obstinacy that I refuse the oath . . . considering that of so many wiser and better men none sticked thereat.'

It was. The government was placed in a quandary. In order to get him, and silence further opposition, it was necessary to stiffen legislation. In November 1534 the Act of Supremacy was passed, making it treason to deny the Royal Supremacy, which had, by the nation's expressed will in Parliament, taken the place of the 'foreign jurisdiction' of the Pope.

17. To Margaret

The Act of Supremacy caught in its toils the few who still held out against the course the nation had decided upon – such as the London Carthusians. And in May 1535 More describes to Margaret the visit of the Privy Councillors to the Tower to make a further effort to gain his subscription.

Our Lord bless you, my dearly beloved daughter. I doubt not but by the reason of the Councillors resorting hither in this time (in which our Lord be their comfort) these Fathers of the Charterhouse and Master Reynolds of Sion that be now judged to death for treason – whose matters and causes I know not – may hap to put you in trouble and fear of mind concerning me, being here prisoner. Specially for that it is not unlikely but that you have heard that I was brought also before the Council here myself . . .

On Friday the last day of April in the afternoon Mr Lieutenant came in here unto me, and showed me that Mr Secretary would speak with

55. *More's Daughter, Margaret Roper*

me. Whereupon I shifted my gown, and went out with Mr Lieutenant into the gallery to him. Where I met many, some known and some unknown in the way . . . Coming into the chamber where his mastership sat with Mr Attorney [Sir Christopher Hales], Mr Solicitor [Sir Richard Rich], Mr Bedyll and Mr Doctor Tregonwell, I was offered to sit with them; which in no wise I would.

Whereupon Mr Secretary . . . doubted not but that I had . . . seen the new statutes made at the last sitting of the Parliament. Whereunto I answered, 'Yea, verily . . .' Then he asked me whether I had not read the first statute of them, of the King being Head of the Church. Whereunto I answered, 'Yes.' Then his mastership declared unto me that – sith it was now by act of Parliament ordained that his highness and his heirs be, and ever right have been, and perpetually should be, Supreme Head of the Church of England under Christ, the King's pleasure was that those of his Council there assembled should demand mine opinion, and what my mind was therein.

Whereunto I answered that in good faith I had well trusted that the King's highness would never have commanded any such question to be demanded of me. Considering that I ever, from the beginning, well and truly . . . declared my mind unto his highness . . . And now I have in good faith discharged my mind of all such matters, and neither will dispute Kings' titles nor Popes' . . .

Whereunto Mr Secretary . . . thought this manner answer should not satisfy nor content the King's highness, but that his grace would

56. *The Duke of Suffolk*

exact a more full answer . . . And that concerning myself, his grace would be glad to see me take such conformable ways as I might be abroad in the world again, among other men, as I have been before.

Whereunto I shortly answered for a very truth that I would never meddle in the world again, to have the world given me . . . Showing that I had fully determined with myself neither to study nor meddle with any matter of this world; but that my whole study should be upon the Passion of Christ, and my own passage out of this world . . .

Mr Secretary said that, though I was prisoner and condemned to perpetual prison, yet I was not thereby discharged of mine obedience and allegiance unto the King's highness. And thereupon demanded me whether that I thought that the King's grace might exact of me such things as are contained in the statutes, and upon like pains, as he might of other men. Whereto I answered that I would not say the contrary.

Whereto he said that, likewise as the King's highness would be gracious to them that he found conformable, so his grace would follow the course of his laws toward such as he shall find obstinate. And his mastership said further that my demeanour in that matter was of a thing that of likelihood made now other men so stiff therein as they be.

Whereto I answered that . . . I could no further go, whatsoever pain should come thereof . . . I do nobody harm, I say none harm, I think none harm, but wish everybody good. And if this be not enough to keep a man alive, in good faith I long not to live. And I am dying already; and have since I came here been divers times in the case that I thought to die within one hour. And I thank our Lord I was never sorry for it, but rather sorry when I saw the pang passed. And therefore my poor body is at the King's pleasure – would God my death might do him good! . . .

18. To Margaret

The government still held its hand, and in June sent yet another commission from the Council to press More for his opinion. He reported the proceedings to Margaret, as usual at great length, qualifying every phrase with his characteristic combination of moral scrupulousness and the repetitious exactitude of the lawyer.

. . . I perceive little difference between this time and the last; for, as far as I can see, the whole purpose is either to drive me to say precisely the one way, or else precisely the other. Here sat my Lord of Canterbury, my Lord Chancellor, my Lord of Suffolk [Henry's brother-in-law], my Lord of Wiltshire [Queen Anne's father], and Mr Secretary [Cromwell] . . . added that the King's highness was nothing content nor satisfied

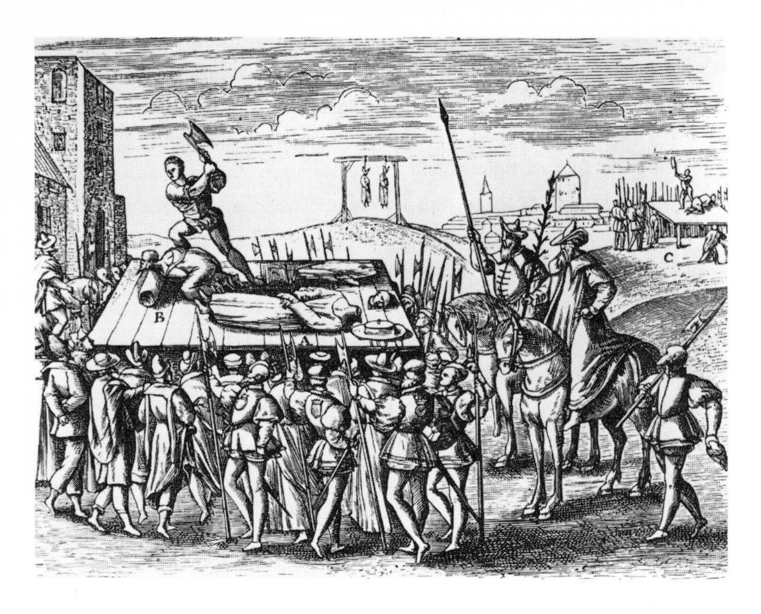

57. *The Scaffold*

with mine answer; but thought that by my demeanour I had been occasion of much grudge and harm in the realm. And that I had an obstinate mind and an evil toward him; and that my duty was, being his subject – and so he had sent them now in his name upon mine allegiance to command me to make a plain and terminate answer: whether I thought the same statute lawful or not. And that I should either acknowledge and confess it lawful that his highness should be Supreme Head of the Church of England, or else to utter plainly my malignity.

Whereunto I answered that I had no malignity, and therefore I could none utter . . . I thanked God that my case was such in this matter, through the clearness of mine own conscience, that, though I might have pain, I could not have harm. For a man may in such case lose his head, and have no harm . . .

To this Mr Secretary said that I had ere this, when I was Chancellor, examined heretics and thieves and other malefactors: and gave me a great praise, above my deserving, in that behalf. And he said that I then – as he thought, and at the leastwise bishops – did use to examine heretics, whether they believed the Pope to be head of the Church, and used to compel them to make a precise answer thereto. And why should not then the King – sith it is a law made here that his grace is head of the Church here – compel men to answer precisely to the law here as they did then concerning the Pope . . . Mr Secretary answered that they were as well burned for the denying of that, as they be beheaded for denying of this; and therefore as good reason to compel them to make precise answer to the one as to the other . . .

Whereto I answered that . . . the reasonableness or the unreasonableness in binding a man to precise answer standeth not in the respect or difference between heading or burning, but because of the difference in charge of conscience between heading and Hell . . . [And] that verily I never purposed to swear any book oath more while I lived.

Then they said that was very obstinate if I would refuse that, for every man doth it in the Star Chamber and everywhere. I said that was true, but I had not so little foresight but that I might well conjecture what should be part of my interrogatory, and as good it was to refuse it at the first, as afterward . . .

In conclusion Mr Secretary said that he liked me this day much worse than he did the last time; for then, he said, he pitied me much, and now he thought that I meant not well. But God and I know both that I mean well, and so I pray God do by me . . .

19. To Margaret

Nothing could be done with More: there was nothing for it but for the government to bring him to open trial in Westminster Hall, the scene of which is the high-light of Roper's biography. Arraigned of high treason, More justified the indictment by at last coming out into the open with his own arraignment of the new deal and the breach with Rome. The scene was marked by one of the most famous snubs in history – More's dressing down of his fellow-lawyer Rich for his perjured evidence. This did not, however, arrest Rich's career: he made a colossal fortune, established himself as Lord Rich in the precincts of Leez priory in Essex, and died in the odour of sanctity as an undeviating Catholic in the Protestant days of Elizabeth, the pious founder of Felsted school.

More's execution took place publicly on Tower Hill – pour décourager les autres *– on 6 July 1535. (Queen Anne's execution – who had driven Henry on – was less than a year away: much less forgivable, for she was no opponent, merely in the way.)*

The day before, More wrote his last letter to his beloved Margaret, from which her husband quotes. Next day was the eve of the translation of the relics of St Thomas of Canterbury: Becket too had wished for martyrdom (as against Eliot's line in Murder in the Cathedral*).*

. . . I cumber you, good Margaret, much; but I should be sorry if it should be any longer than tomorrow; for it is St Thomas' Eve, and the utas [octave] of St Peter. And therefore tomorrow long I to go to God: it were a day very meet and convenient for me.

ACKNOWLEDGEMENTS

The publishers would like to thank those listed below for permission to reproduce the illustrations indicated, or for supplying photographic material.

Her Majesty the Queen 4, 10, 30, 31, 32, 38, 44, 48; Ashmolean Museum 28, 40, 51; Biblioteca Apostolica Vaticana 46; Bodleian Library, Oxford 41; British Library Board 49; City of Bristol Museum and Art Gallery 45; Galleria Nazionale d'Arte Antica, Rome 8; Mansell Collection 5, 9, 15, 16, 19, 21, 24, 29, 39; Metropolitan Museum of Art, New York 2, 55; Museo del Prado, Madrid 43; National Portrait Gallery 1, 3, 6, 14, 20, 22, 25, 27, 33, 47, 50, 52, 53, 56; Radio Times Hulton Picture Library 11, 35, 54, 57; Royal College of Arms 17, 18; Thyssen Collection 26; Trustees of Lambeth Palace Library 12; Trustees of the British Museum 7, 34, 37, 42; Victoria and Albert Museum 13, 23; Weidenfeld and Nicholson 36.